HOUGHTON MIFFLIN HARCOURT

MATH
Expressions
Common Core

Dr. Karen C. Fuson

GRADE

3

Volume 1

This material is based upon work supported by the
National Science Foundation
under Grant Numbers
ESI-9816320, REC-9806020, and RED-935373.

Any opinions, findings, and conclusions, or recommendations expressed in this material
are those of the author and do not necessarily reflect the views of the National Science Foundation.

 HOUGHTON MIFFLIN HARCOURT

ISBN: 978-0-547-82423-9

6 7 8 9 10   0982   21 20 19 18 17 16 15 14 13

4500427626   B C D E F G

Homework

Name _____ Date _____

Home Study Sheet A

5s

Count-bys	Mixed Up ×	Mixed Up ÷
$1 \times 5 = 5$	$2 \times 5 = 10$	$10 \div 5 = 2$
$2 \times 5 = 10$	$9 \times 5 = 45$	$35 \div 5 = 7$
$3 \times 5 = 15$	$1 \times 5 = 5$	$50 \div 5 = 10$
$4 \times 5 = 20$	$5 \times 5 = 25$	$5 \div 5 = 1$
$5 \times 5 = 25$	$7 \times 5 = 35$	$20 \div 5 = 4$
$6 \times 5 = 30$	$3 \times 5 = 15$	$15 \div 5 = 3$
$7 \times 5 = 35$	$10 \times 5 = 50$	$30 \div 5 = 6$
$8 \times 5 = 40$	$6 \times 5 = 30$	$40 \div 5 = 8$
$9 \times 5 = 45$	$4 \times 5 = 20$	$25 \div 5 = 5$
$10 \times 5 = 50$	$8 \times 5 = 40$	$45 \div 5 = 9$

2s

Count-bys	Mixed Up ×	Mixed Up ÷
$1 \times 2 = 2$	$7 \times 2 = 14$	$20 \div 2 = 10$
$2 \times 2 = 4$	$1 \times 2 = 2$	$2 \div 2 = 1$
$3 \times 2 = 6$	$3 \times 2 = 6$	$6 \div 2 = 3$
$4 \times 2 = 8$	$5 \times 2 = 10$	$16 \div 2 = 8$
$5 \times 2 = 10$	$6 \times 2 = 12$	$12 \div 2 = 6$
$6 \times 2 = 12$	$8 \times 2 = 16$	$4 \div 2 = 2$
$7 \times 2 = 14$	$2 \times 2 = 4$	$10 \div 2 = 5$
$8 \times 2 = 16$	$10 \times 2 = 20$	$8 \div 2 = 4$
$9 \times 2 = 18$	$4 \times 2 = 8$	$14 \div 2 = 7$
$10 \times 2 = 20$	$9 \times 2 = 18$	$18 \div 2 = 9$

10s

Count-bys	Mixed Up ×	Mixed Up ÷
$1 \times 10 = 10$	$1 \times 10 = 10$	$80 \div 10 = 8$
$2 \times 10 = 20$	$5 \times 10 = 50$	$10 \div 10 = 1$
$3 \times 10 = 30$	$2 \times 10 = 20$	$50 \div 10 = 5$
$4 \times 10 = 40$	$8 \times 10 = 80$	$90 \div 10 = 9$
$5 \times 10 = 50$	$7 \times 10 = 70$	$40 \div 10 = 4$
$6 \times 10 = 60$	$3 \times 10 = 30$	$100 \div 10 = 10$
$7 \times 10 = 70$	$4 \times 10 = 40$	$30 \div 10 = 3$
$8 \times 10 = 80$	$6 \times 10 = 60$	$20 \div 10 = 2$
$9 \times 10 = 90$	$10 \times 10 = 100$	$70 \div 10 = 7$
$10 \times 10 = 100$	$9 \times 10 = 90$	$60 \div 10 = 6$

9s

Count-bys	Mixed Up ×	Mixed Up ÷
$1 \times 9 = 9$	$2 \times 9 = 18$	$81 \div 9 = 9$
$2 \times 9 = 18$	$4 \times 9 = 36$	$18 \div 9 = 2$
$3 \times 9 = 27$	$7 \times 9 = 63$	$36 \div 9 = 4$
$4 \times 9 = 36$	$8 \times 9 = 72$	$9 \div 9 = 1$
$5 \times 9 = 45$	$3 \times 9 = 27$	$54 \div 9 = 6$
$6 \times 9 = 54$	$10 \times 9 = 90$	$27 \div 9 = 3$
$7 \times 9 = 63$	$1 \times 9 = 9$	$63 \div 9 = 7$
$8 \times 9 = 72$	$6 \times 9 = 54$	$72 \div 9 = 8$
$9 \times 9 = 81$	$5 \times 9 = 45$	$90 \div 9 = 10$
$10 \times 9 = 90$	$9 \times 9 = 81$	$45 \div 9 = 5$

Homework

Home Signature Sheet

	Count-Bys Homework Helper	Multiplications Homework Helper	Divisions Homework Helper
0			
1			
2			
3			
4			
5			
6			
7			
8			
9			
10			

Homework

Use this chart to practice your 5s count-bys, multiplications, and divisions. Then have your Homework Helper test you.

	In Order ×	Mixed Up ×	Mixed Up ÷
5s	$1 \times 5 = 5$	$4 \times 5 = 20$	$20 \div 5 = 4$
	$2 \times 5 = 10$	$7 \times 5 = 35$	$5 \div 5 = 1$
	$3 \times 5 = 15$	$2 \times 5 = 10$	$50 \div 5 = 10$
	$4 \times 5 = 20$	$5 \times 5 = 25$	$35 \div 5 = 7$
	$5 \times 5 = 25$	$9 \times 5 = 45$	$15 \div 5 = 3$
	$6 \times 5 = 30$	$1 \times 5 = 5$	$45 \div 5 = 9$
	$7 \times 5 = 35$	$10 \times 5 = 50$	$10 \div 5 = 2$
	$8 \times 5 = 40$	$3 \times 5 = 15$	$25 \div 5 = 5$
	$9 \times 5 = 45$	$6 \times 5 = 30$	$40 \div 5 = 8$
	$10 \times 5 = 50$	$8 \times 5 = 40$	$30 \div 5 = 6$

Homework

Multiply or divide to find the unknown numbers.
Then check your answers at the bottom of this page.

1. $5 \times 6 = \boxed{}$

2. $45 \div 5 = \boxed{}$

3. $5 \times \boxed{} = 35$

4. $\boxed{} \times 5 = 10$

5. $3 \times 5 = \boxed{}$

6. $50 / 5 = \boxed{}$

$5 \cdot 9 = \boxed{}$

8. $\boxed{} \cdot 5 = 20$

9. $5\overline{)25}$

10. $\boxed{} * \boxed{} = 40$

11. $5 \cdot 5 = \boxed{}$

12. $\dfrac{35}{5} = \boxed{}$

13. $5 \boxed{} = 15$

14. $30 \div 5 = \boxed{}$

15. $5 \times \boxed{} = 45$

16. $\boxed{} \div 5 = 7$

17. $\dfrac{10}{5} = \boxed{}$

18. $5 \cdot 8 = \boxed{}$

19. $5\overline{)20}$

20. $5 \times \boxed{} = 5$

21. $5 \times \boxed{} = 50$

1. 30 2. 9 3. 7 4. 2 5. 15 6. 10 7. 45 8. 4 9. 5 10. 8 11. 25
12. 7 13. 3 14. 6 15. 9 16. 35 17. 2 18. 40 19. 4 20. 1 21. 10

The Meaning of Division

Name \   **Date**

Homework

Use this chart to practice your 2s count-bys, multiplications, and divisions. Then have your Homework Helper test you.

	× In Order	× Mixed Up	÷ Mixed Up
2s	$1 \times 2 = 2$	$4 \times 2 = 8$	$18 \div 2 = 9$
	$2 \times 2 = 4$	$7 \times 2 = 14$	$6 \div 2 = 3$
	$3 \times 2 = 6$	$2 \times 2 = 4$	$2 \div 2 = 1$
	$4 \times 2 = 8$	$5 \times 2 = 10$	$16 \div 2 = 8$
	$5 \times 2 = 10$	$9 \times 2 = 18$	$14 \div 2 = 7$
	$6 \times 2 = 12$	$1 \times 2 = 2$	$4 \div 2 = 2$
	$7 \times 2 = 14$	$10 \times 2 = 20$	$20 \div 2 = 10$
	$8 \times 2 = 16$	$3 \times 2 = 6$	$8 \div 2 = 4$
	$9 \times 2 = 18$	$6 \times 2 = 12$	$12 \div 2 = 6$
	$10 \times 2 = 20$	$8 \times 2 = 16$	$10 \div 2 = 5$

Homework

Name _____ **Date** _____

Multiply or divide to find the unknown numbers. Then check your answers at the bottom of this page.

1. $2 \times 4 = \boxed{}$

2. $20 \div 5 = \boxed{}$

3. $6 * 2 = \boxed{}$

4. $45 / 5 = \boxed{}$

5. $2 \cdot 10 = \boxed{}$

6. $\dfrac{20}{2} = \boxed{}$

7. $5 \times 10 = \boxed{}$

8. $16 \div 2 = \boxed{}$

9. $6 \times 5 = \boxed{}$

10. $30 / 5 = \boxed{}$

11. $5 \cdot 7 = \boxed{}$

12. $2\overline{)18}$ with $\boxed{}$

13. $8 * 2 = \boxed{}$

14. $\dfrac{25}{5} = \boxed{}$

15. $5 \cdot 4 = \boxed{}$

16. $16 / 2 = \boxed{}$

17. $2\overline{)10}$ with $\boxed{}$

18. $2 * 7 = \boxed{}$

19. $5 \times 5 = \boxed{}$

20. $14 \div 2 = \boxed{}$

21. $\dfrac{\boxed{}}{5} = 7$

12. 9   13. 16   14. 5   15. 20   16. 8   17. 5   18. 14   19. 25   20. 7   21. 35

1. 8   2. 4   3. 12   4. 9   5. 20   6. 10   7. 50   8. 8   9. 30   10. 6   11. 35

Multiply and Divide with 2

© Houghton Mifflin Harcourt Publishing Company

Homework

Home Check Sheet 1: 5s and 2s

5s Multiplication	5s Divisions	2s Multiplications	2s Divisions
2 × 5 = 10	30 / 5 = 6	4 × 2 = 8	8 / 2 = 4
5 • 6 = 30	5 ÷ 5 = 1	2 • 8 = 16	18 ÷ 2 = 9
5 * 9 = 45	15 / 5 = 3	1 * 2 = 2	2 / 2 = 1
4 × 5 = 20	50 ÷ 5 = 10	6 × 2 = 12	16 ÷ 2 = 8
5 • 7 = 35	20 / 5 = 4	2 • 9 = 18	4 / 2 = 2
10 * 5 = 50	10 ÷ 5 = 2	2 * 2 = 4	20 ÷ 2 = 10
1 × 5 = 5	35 / 5 =	3 × 2 = 6	10 / 2 = 5
5 • 3 = 15	40 ÷ 5 = 8	2 • 5 = 10	12 ÷ 2 = 6
8 * 5 = 40	25 / 5 = 5	10 * 2 = 20	6 / 2 = 3
5 × 5 = 25	45 / 5 = 9	× 7 = 14	14 / 2 = 7
5 • 8 = 40	20 ÷ 5 = 4	2 • 10 = 20	4 ÷ 2 = 2
7 * 5 = 35	15 / 5 = 3	9 * 2 = 18	2 / 2 = 1
5 × 4 = 20	30 ÷ 5 = 6	2 × 6 = 12	8 ÷ 2 = 4
6 • 5 = 30	25 / 5 = 5	8 • 2 = 16	6 / 2 = 3
5 * 1 = 5	10 ÷ 5 = 2	2 * 3 =	20 ÷ 2 = 10
5 × 10 = 50	45 / 5 = 9	2 × 2 = 4	14 / 2 = 7
9 • 5 = 45	35 ÷ 5 = 7	1 • 2 = 2	10 ÷ 2 = 5
5 * 2 = 10	50 ÷ 5 = 10	2 * 4 = 8	16 ÷ 2 = 8
3 × 5 = 15	40 / 5 = 8	5 × 2 = 10	12 / 2 = 6
5 • 5 = 25	5 ÷ 5 = 1	7 • 2 = 14	18 ÷ 2 = 9

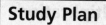
Study Plan

Homework Helper

Write an equation and solve the problem.

1. Tanya had 14 cups to fill with juice. She put them in 2 equal rows. How many cups were in each row?

2. Rebecca has 3 pairs of running shoes. She bought new shoelaces for each pair. How many shoelaces did she buy?

3. Jason served his family dinner. He put 5 carrots on each of the 4 plates. How many carrots did Jason serve in all?

4. Olivia filled 8 vases with flowers. She put 5 flowers in each vase. How many flowers did she put in the vases?

5. Devon has 30 model airplanes. He put the same number on each of the 5 shelves of his bookcase. How many model airplanes did Devon put on each shelf?

6. There are 12 eggs in a carton. They are arranged in 2 rows with the same number of eggs in each row. How many eggs are in each row?

Name _____ **Date** _____

Remembering

Make a math drawing for the problem and label it with a multiplication equation. Then write the answer to the problem.

1. Kishore has 4 stacks with 3 books in each stack. How many books are there in all?

   _____

2. Cindy had 6 envelopes. She put 2 stamps on each one. How many stamps did she use?

   _____

Write a multiplication equation for the array.

3. How many dots?

   _____

Multiply or divide to find the unknown numbers.

4. $7 * 5 = \boxed{}$

5. $45 \div 5 = \boxed{}$

6. $\boxed{} \times 5 = 50$

7. $8 * 5 = \boxed{}$

8. $5 \bullet \boxed{} = 25$

9. $\dfrac{10}{5} = \boxed{}$

10. **Stretch Your Thinking** Explain how to solve the following problem using division and multiplication. There are 18 students in the classroom. There are 2 students in each group. How many groups of students are there?

    _____

    _____

Name _____ **Date** _____

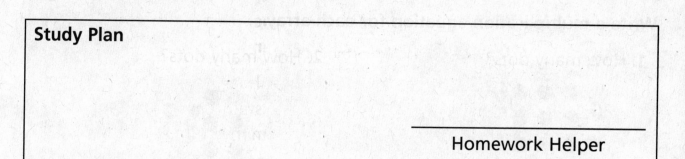

Homework

Study Plan

_____

Homework Helper

Write an equation and solve the problem.

1. On a wall, photos are arranged in 2 rows with 7 photos in each row. How many photos are on the wall?

_____

2. An orchard has 6 rows of apple trees. Each row has 5 trees. How many apple trees are in the orchard?

_____

3. Navin arranged his soccer trophies into 5 equal rows. He has 25 trophies. How many are in each row?

_____

4. Tickets to the school play cost $2 each. Mrs. Cortez spent $16 on tickets. How many tickets did she buy?

_____

5. Jimet solved 20 multiplications. There were 5 multiplications in each row. How many rows of multiplications did she solve?

_____

6. Josh has 2 peaches for each of his 6 friends. How many peaches does he have?

_____

Name _____   Date _____

Remembering

Write a multiplication equation for each array.

1. How many dots?

2. How many dots?

_____   _____

Multiply or divide to find the unknown numbers.

3. $2 \times 7 = \boxed{}$

4. $5 \bullet \boxed{} = 30$

5. $5\overline{)5}^{\boxed{}}$

6. $25 \div 5 = \boxed{}$

7. $4 * 5 = \boxed{}$

8. $\frac{35}{5} = \boxed{}$

Write an equation and solve the problem.

9. There are 10 sunglasses on the display. Each has 2 lenses. How many lenses are there?

_____

10. Bryce draws 40 stars on his poster. He draws 5 rows and puts the same number in each row. How many stars are in each row?

_____

11. Stretch Your Thinking Sarah has 10 stuffed animals. Explain two different ways she can group the stuffed animals so each group has the same number and no stuffed animals are left over.

_____

_____

Building Fluency with 2s and 5s

Use this chart to practice your 10s count-bys, multiplications, and divisions. Then have your Homework Helper test you.

	× In Order	× Mixed Up	÷ Mixed Up
10s	$1 \times 10 = 10$	$4 \times 10 = 40$	$100 \div 10 = 10$
	$2 \times 10 = 20$	$7 \times 10 = 70$	$20 \div 10 = 2$
	$3 \times 10 = 30$	$2 \times 10 = 20$	$40 \div 10 = 4$
	$4 \times 10 = 40$	$5 \times 10 = 50$	$70 \div 10 = 7$
	$5 \times 10 = 50$	$9 \times 10 = 90$	$30 \div 10 = 3$
	$6 \times 10 = 60$	$1 \times 10 = 10$	$60 \div 10 = 6$
	$7 \times 10 = 70$	$10 \times 10 = 100$	$80 \div 10 = 8$
	$8 \times 10 = 80$	$3 \times 10 = 30$	$10 \div 10 = 1$
	$9 \times 10 = 90$	$6 \times 10 = 60$	$50 \div 10 = 5$
	$10 \times 10 = 100$	$8 \times 10 = 80$	$90 \div 10 = 9$

Homework

Multiply or divide to find the unknown numbers. Then check your answers at the bottom of this page.

1. $2 \times 10 = \boxed{}$

2. $15 \div 5 = \boxed{}$

3. $4 * 2 = \boxed{}$

4. $80 / 10 = \boxed{}$

5. $5 \bullet \boxed{} = 40$

6. $\frac{60}{10} = \boxed{}$

7. $\boxed{} \times 5 = 30$

8. $\frac{20}{2} = \boxed{}$

9. $6 \times 10 = \boxed{}$

10. $25 / 5 = \boxed{}$

11. $10 \bullet 7 = \boxed{}$

12. $14 \div 2 = \boxed{}$

13. $9 * 2 = \boxed{}$

14. $\frac{45}{5} = \boxed{}$

15. $10 \bullet 4 = \boxed{}$

16. $2\overline{)20}$ with $\boxed{}$ above

17. $70 \div 10 = \boxed{}$

18. $9 * \boxed{} = 18$

19. $\boxed{} \times 5 = 35$

20. $\frac{\boxed{}}{3} = 10$

21. $\boxed{} \bullet 2 = 16$

1.20 2.3 3.8 4.8 5.8 6.6 7.6 8.10 9.60 10.5 11.70 12.7 13.18 14.9 15.40 16.10 17.7 18.2 19.7 20.30 21.8

Multiply and Divide with 10

Homework

Use this chart to practice your 9s count-bys, multiplications, and divisions. Then have your Homework Helper test you.

	× In Order	× Mixed Up	÷ Mixed Up
9s	$1 \times 9 = 9$	$4 \times 9 = 36$	$63 \div 9 = 7$
	$2 \times 9 = 18$	$7 \times 9 = 63$	$9 \div 9 = 1$
	$3 \times 9 = 27$	$2 \times 9 = 18$	$54 \div 9 = 6$
	$4 \times 9 = 36$	$5 \times 9 = 45$	$18 \div 9 = 2$
	$5 \times 9 = 45$	$9 \times 9 = 81$	$90 \div 9 = 10$
	$6 \times 9 = 54$	$1 \times 9 = 9$	$81 \div 9 = 9$
	$7 \times 9 = 63$	$10 \times 9 = 90$	$45 \div 9 = 5$
	$8 \times 9 = 72$	$3 \times 9 = 27$	$27 \div 9 = 3$
	$9 \times 9 = 81$	$6 \times 9 = 54$	$36 \div 9 = 4$
	$10 \times 9 = 90$	$8 \times 9 = 72$	$72 \div 9 = 8$

Homework

Multiply or divide to find the unknown numbers. Then check your answers at the bottom of this page.

1. $2 \times 9 = \boxed{}$

2. $18 \div 2 = \boxed{}$

3. $6 * \boxed{} = 12$

4. $40 / 5 = \boxed{}$

5. $10 \bullet 8 = \boxed{}$

6. $\frac{27}{9} = \boxed{}$

7. $\boxed{} \times 5 = 40$

8. $2\overline{)14}$ with $\boxed{}$ above

9. $9 \times 10 = \boxed{}$

10. $\frac{60}{10} = \boxed{}$

11. $10 \bullet 7 = \boxed{}$

12. $72 \div 9 = \boxed{}$

13. $5 * 9 = \boxed{}$

14. $\frac{20}{2} = \boxed{}$

15. $9 \bullet \boxed{} = 36$

16. $10 / 2 = \boxed{}$

17. $63 \div 9 = \boxed{}$

18. $9 * 9 = \boxed{}$

19. $5 \times 5 = \boxed{}$

20. $5\overline{)30}$ with $\boxed{}$ above

21. $9 \times 3 = \boxed{}$

1. 18 **2.** 9 **3.** 2 **4.** 8 **5.** 80 **6.** 3 **7.** 8 **8.** 7 **9.** 90 **10.** 6 **11.** 70
12. 8 **13.** 45 **14.** 10 **15.** 4 **16.** 5 **17.** 7 **18.** 81 **19.** 25 **20.** 6 **21.** 27

Multiply and Divide with 9

Name _____

Date _____

Home Check Sheet 2: 10s and 9s

10s Multiplications	10s Divisions	9s Multiplications	9s Divisions
$9 \times 10 = 90$	$100 / 10 = 10$	$3 \times 9 = 27$	$27 / 9 = 3$
$10 \cdot 3 = 30$	$50 \div 10 = 5$	$9 \cdot 7 = 63$	$9 \div 9 = 1$
$10 * 6 = 60$	$70 / 10 = 7$	$10 * 9 = 90$	$81 / 9 = 9$
$1 \times 10 = 10$	$40 \div 10 = 4$	$5 \times 9 = 45$	$45 \div 9 = 5$
$10 \cdot 4 = 40$	$80 / 10 = 8$	$9 \cdot 8 = 72$	$90 / 9 = 10$
$10 * 7 = 70$	$60 \div 10 = 6$	$9 * 1 = 9$	$36 \div 9 = 4$
$8 \times 10 = 80$	$10 / 10 = 1$	$2 \times 9 = 18$	$18 / 9 = 2$
$10 \cdot 10 = 100$	$20 \div 10 = 2$	$9 \cdot 9 = 81$	$63 \div 9 = 7$
$5 * 10 = 50$	$90 / 10 = 9$	$6 * 9 = 54$	$54 / 9 = 6$
$10 \times 2 = 20$	$30 / 10 = 3$	$9 \times 4 = 36$	$72 / 9 = 8$
$10 \cdot 5 = 50$	$80 \div 10 = 8$	$9 \cdot 5 = 45$	$27 \div 9 = 3$
$4 * 10 = 40$	$70 / 10 = 7$	$4 * 9 = 36$	$45 / 9 = 5$
$10 \times 1 = 10$	$100 \div 10 = 10$	$9 \times 1 = 9$	$63 \div 9 = 7$
$3 \cdot 10 = 30$	$90 / 10 = 9$	$3 \cdot 9 = 27$	$72 / 9 = 8$
$10 * 8 = 80$	$60 \div 10 = 6$	$9 * 8 = 72$	$54 \div 9 = 6$
$7 \times 10 = 70$	$30 / 10 = 3$	$7 \times 9 = 63$	$18 / 9 = 2$
$6 \cdot 10 = 60$	$10 \div 10 = 1$	$6 \cdot 9 = 54$	$90 \div 9 = 10$
$10 * 9 = 90$	$40 \div 10 = 4$	$9 * 9 = 81$	$9 \div 9 = 1$
$10 \times 10 = 100$	$20 / 10 = 2$	$10 \times 9 = 90$	$36 / 9 = 4$
$2 \cdot 10 = 20$	$50 \div 10 = 5$	$2 \cdot 9 = 18$	$81 \div 9 = 9$

Homework

Home Check Sheet 3: 2s, 5s, 9s, and 10s

2s, 5s, 9s,10s Multiplications	2s, 5s, 9s, 10s Multiplications	2s, 5s, 9s, 10s Divisions	2s, 5s, 9s, 10s Divisions
$2 \times 10 = 20$	$5 \times 10 = 50$	$18 / 2 = 9$	$36 / 9 = 4$
$10 \cdot 5 = 50$	$10 \cdot 9 = 90$	$50 \div 5 = 10$	$70 \div 10 = 7$
$9 * 6 = 54$	$4 * 10 = 40$	$72 / 9 = 8$	$18 / 2 = 9$
$7 \times 10 = 70$	$2 \times 9 = 18$	$60 \div 10 = 6$	$45 \div 5 = 9$
$2 \cdot 3 = 6$	$5 \cdot 3 = 15$	$12 / 2 = 6$	$45 / 9 = 5$
$5 * 7 = 35$	$6 * 9 = 54$	$30 \div 5 = 6$	$30 \div 10 = 3$
$9 \times 10 = 90$	$10 \times 3 = 30$	$18 / 9 = 2$	$6 / 2 = 3$
$6 \cdot 10 = 60$	$3 \cdot 2 = 6$	$50 \div 10 = 5$	$50 \div 5 = 10$
$8 * 2 = 16$	$5 * 8 = 40$	$14 / 2 = 7$	$27 / 9 = 3$
$5 \times 6 = 30$	$9 \times 9 = 81$	$25 / 5 = 5$	$70 / 10 = 7$
$9 \cdot 5 = 45$	$10 \cdot 4 = 40$	$81 \div 9 = 9$	$20 \div 2 = 10$
$8 * 10 = 80$	$9 * 2 = 18$	$20 / 10 = 2$	$45 / 5 = 9$
$2 \times 1 = 2$	$5 \times 1 = 5$	$8 \div 2 = 4$	$54 \div 9 = 6$
$3 \cdot 5 = 15$	$9 \cdot 6 = 54$	$45 / 5 = 9$	$80 / 10 = 8$
$4 * 9 = 36$	$10 * 1 = 10$	$63 \div 9 = 7$	$16 \div 2 = 8$
$3 \times 10 = 30$	$7 \times 2 = 14$	$30 / 10 = 3$	$15 / 5 = 3$
$2 \cdot 6 = 12$	$6 \cdot 5 = 30$	$10 \div 2 = 5$	$90 \div 9 = 10$
$4 * 5 = 20$	$8 * 9 = 72$	$40 \div 5 = 8$	$100 \div 10 = 10$
$9 \times 7 = 63$	$10 \times 6 = 60$	$9 / 9 = 1$	$12 / 2 = 6$
$1 \cdot 10 = 10$	$2 \cdot 8 = 16$	$50 \div 10 = 5$	$35 \div 5 = 7$

Homework

Multiply or divide to find the unknown numbers. Then check your answers at the bottom of this page.

1. $5 \times 6 = \boxed{}$ **2.** $50 \div 10 = \boxed{}$ **3.** $6 * 9 = \boxed{}$

4. $12 / 2 = \boxed{}$ **5.** $9 \times \boxed{} = 72$ **6.** $\dfrac{14}{2} = \boxed{}$

7. $ \bullet 5 = \boxed{}$ **8.** $15 \div 5 = \boxed{}$ **9.** $7 \times 2 = \boxed{}$

10. $ / 5 = \boxed{}$ **11.** $10 \bullet \boxed{} = 40$ **12.** $9\overline{)27}$ $\boxed{}$

13. $ = \boxed{}$ **14.** $\dfrac{81}{9} = \boxed{}$ **15.** $7 \bullet \boxed{} = 35$

16.   **17.** $10 \div \boxed{} = 5$ **18.** $2 * 7 = \boxed{}$

19. $\boxed{}$ **20.** $2 \times 7 = \boxed{}$ **21.** $18 / 2 = \boxed{}$

1. 30 **2.** 5 **3.** 54 **4.** 6 **5.** 8 **6.** 7 **7.** 45 **8.** 3 **9.** 14 **10.** **11.** **12.** 3 **13.** 40 **14.** 9 **15.** 5 **16.** 10 **17.** 2 **18.** 14 **19.** 6

Name _____ **Date** _____

Study Plan

Homework Helper

Write an equation for each situation. Then solve the problem.

1. Quinn rode his bike 35 miles. He stopped for water every 5 miles. How many times did Quinn stop for water?

_____

2. Roy had 12 bottles of juice. He put them in the refrigerator in 2 rows. How many bottles were in each row?

_____

3. Melinda has 5 cousins. She called each one on the phone 4 times this month. How many phone calls did she make to her cousins this month?

_____

4. Janelle won 27 tickets at the fair. She traded the tickets for 9 prizes. Each prize was worth the same number of tickets. How many tickets was each prize worth?

_____

5. Eric had 2 picnic baskets. He put 7 apples in each one. How many apples did he put into the picnic baskets?

_____

6. Grace has read 2 chapters in each of her 9 books. How many chapters has she read in all?

_____

Remembering

Write an equation and solve the problem.

1. Maria wants some pens that cost $2 each. She spends $12 on pens. How many pens does she buy?

_____

2. Mrs. Lee has 5 crayons for each of her 10 students. How many crayons does Mrs. Lee have?

_____

Multiply or divide to find the unknown numbers.

3. $5 \cdot 1 = \boxed{}$

4. $2 \times \boxed{} = 8$

5. $\dfrac{90}{10} = \boxed{}$

6. $30 \div 10 = \boxed{}$

7. $2 \overline{)14}$

8. $\boxed{} * 5 = 35$

Write an equation and solve the problem.

9. The art teacher has 63 paintbrushes. There are 9 paintbrushes in each box. How many boxes are there?

_____

10. There are 8 plates. Jamie puts 9 strawberries on each plate. How many strawberries are on the plates?

_____

11. Mr. Kim receives an order of 30 new books for the media center. He displays the same number of books on each of 5 shelves. How many books are on each shelf?

_____

12. **Stretch Your Thinking** Write a word problem using 9 and 10 as factors. Write an equation to solve your problem.

_____

_____

Homework

Use this chart to practice your 3s count-bys, multiplications, and divisions. Then have your Homework Helper test you.

	× In Order	× Mixed Up	÷ Mixed Up
3s	$1 \times 3 = 3$	$3 \times 3 = 9$	$27 \div 3 = 9$
	$2 \times 3 = 6$	$5 \times 3 = 15$	$21 \div 3 = 7$
	$3 \times 3 = 9$	$1 \times 3 = 3$	$3 \div 3 = 1$
	$4 \times 3 = 12$	$8 \times 3 = 24$	$9 \div 3 = 3$
	$5 \times 3 = 15$	$2 \times 3 = 6$	$30 \div 3 = 10$
	$6 \times 3 = 18$	$9 \times 3 = 27$	$24 \div 3 = 8$
	$7 \times 3 = 21$	$7 \times 3 = 21$	$12 \div 3 = 4$
	$8 \times 3 = 24$	$10 \times 3 = 30$	$6 \div 3 = 2$
	$9 \times 3 = 27$	$6 \times 3 = 18$	$15 \div 3 = 5$
	$10 \times 3 = 30$	$4 \times 3 = 12$	$18 \div 3 = 6$

Homework

Multiply or divide to find the unknown numbers. Then check your answers at the bottom of this page.

1. $6 \times 3 = \boxed{}$

2. $3\overline{)27}$ (quotient box above)

3. $2 * \boxed{} = 18$

4. $18 / 9 = \boxed{}$

5. $3 \times \boxed{} = 30$

6. $\frac{15}{3} = \boxed{}$

7. $9 \cdot 8 = \boxed{}$

8. $50 \div 10 = \boxed{}$

9. $2 \times 2 = \boxed{}$

10. $35 / 5 = \boxed{}$

11. $4 \cdot 10 = \boxed{}$

12. $14 \div 2 = \boxed{}$

13. $8 * 3 = \boxed{}$

14. $\frac{63}{9} = \boxed{}$

15. $5 \cdot \boxed{} = 35$

16. $9\overline{)27}$ (quotient box above)

17. $10 \div \boxed{} = 2$

18. $\boxed{} * 9 = 18$

19. $5 \times 9 = \boxed{}$

20. $81 \div \boxed{} = 9$

21. $14 / 2 = \boxed{}$

1. 18 2. 9 3. 9 4. 2 5. 10 6. 5 7. 72 8. 5 9. 4 10. 7 11. 40
12. 7 13. 24 14. 7 15. 7 16. 3 17. 5 18. 2 19. 45 20. 9 21. 7

Multiply and Divide with 3

2×2

$\begin{array}{r} 2 \\ \times\ 3 \\ \hline \end{array}$ $\begin{array}{r} 3 \\ \times\ 2 \\ \hline \end{array}$

2×4
4×2

$\begin{array}{r} 2 \\ \times\ 5 \\ \hline \end{array}$ $\begin{array}{r} 5 \\ \times\ 2 \\ \hline \end{array}$

2×6
6×2

$\begin{array}{r} 2 \\ \times\ 7 \\ \hline \end{array}$ $\begin{array}{r} 7 \\ \times\ 2 \\ \hline \end{array}$

2×8
8×2

$\begin{array}{r} 2 \\ \times\ 9 \\ \hline \end{array}$ $\begin{array}{r} 9 \\ \times\ 2 \\ \hline \end{array}$

$10 = 2 \times 5$
$10 = 5 \times 2$

5
10
2
4
6
8
10

5
2 : 10

2
$\times 4$
8

4
$\times 2$
8

2
4
6
8

4
8

2
4 : 8

$6 = 2 \times 3$
$6 = 3 \times 2$

3
6
2
4
6

3
2 : 6

2
$\times 2$
4

2
4

2
2 : 4

$18 = 2 \times 9$
$18 = 9 \times 2$

9
18
2
4
6
8
10
12
14
16
18

9
2 : 18

2
$\times 8$
16

8
$\times 2$
16

8
16

2
4
6
8
10
12
14
16

2
8 : 16

$14 = 2 \times 7$
$14 = 7 \times 2$

7
14
2
4
6
8
10
12
14

7
2 : 14

2
$\times 6$
12

6
$\times 2$
12

6
12

2
4
6
8
10
12

2
6 : 12

Home Multiplication Strategy Cards

3×3

$$\begin{array}{r} 3 \\ \times 4 \\ \hline \end{array} \qquad \begin{array}{r} 4 \\ \times 3 \\ \hline \end{array}$$

3×5
5×3

$$\begin{array}{r} 3 \\ \times 6 \\ \hline \end{array} \qquad \begin{array}{r} 6 \\ \times 3 \\ \hline \end{array}$$

3×7
7×3

$$\begin{array}{r} 3 \\ \times 8 \\ \hline \end{array} \qquad \begin{array}{r} 8 \\ \times 3 \\ \hline \end{array}$$

3×9
9×3

$$\begin{array}{r} 4 \\ \times 4 \\ \hline \end{array}$$

Home Multiplication Strategy Cards **43**

$18 = 3 \times 6$

$18 = 6 \times 3$

6	3
12	6
18	9
	12
	15
	18

6
3 ○○○○○ **18**

$\begin{array}{r} 3 \\ \times 5 \\ \hline 15 \end{array}$ $\begin{array}{r} 5 \\ \times 3 \\ \hline 15 \end{array}$

5	3
10	6
15	9
	12
	15

3
5 ○ **15**

$12 = 3 \times 4$

$12 = 4 \times 3$

4	3
8	6
12	9
	12

4
3 ○○○ **12**

$\begin{array}{r} 3 \\ \times 3 \\ \hline 9 \end{array}$

3
6
9

3
3 ○○ **9**

$16 = 4 \times 4$

4
8
12
16

4
4 ○ **16**

$\begin{array}{r} 3 \\ \times 9 \\ \hline 27 \end{array}$ $\begin{array}{r} 9 \\ \times 3 \\ \hline 27 \end{array}$

9	3
18	6
27	9
	12
	15
	18
	21
	24
	27

9
3 ○ **27**

$24 = 3 \times 8$

$24 = 8 \times 3$

8	3
16	6
24	9
	12
	15
	18
	21
	24

3
8 ○ **24**

$\begin{array}{r} 3 \\ \times 7 \\ \hline 21 \end{array}$ $\begin{array}{r} 7 \\ \times 3 \\ \hline 21 \end{array}$

7	3
14	6
21	9
	12
	15
	18
	21

7
3 ○ **21**

Home Multiplication Strategy Cards

4×5
5×4

$$\begin{array}{r} 4 \\ \times 6 \\ \hline \end{array} \qquad \begin{array}{r} 6 \\ \times 4 \\ \hline \end{array}$$

4×7
7×4

$$\begin{array}{r} 4 \\ \times 8 \\ \hline \end{array} \qquad \begin{array}{r} 8 \\ \times 4 \\ \hline \end{array}$$

4×9
9×4

$$\begin{array}{r} 5 \\ \times 5 \\ \hline \end{array}$$

5×6
6×5

$$\begin{array}{r} 5 \\ \times 7 \\ \hline \end{array} \qquad \begin{array}{r} 7 \\ \times 5 \\ \hline \end{array}$$

$32 = 4 \times 8$

$32 = 8 \times 4$

8	4
16	8
24	12
32	16
	20
	24
	28
	32

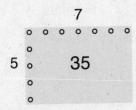

4

8 32

---

4 × 7 = 28

7 × 4 = 28

7	4
14	8
21	12
28	16
	20
	24
	28

7

4 28

$24 = 4 \times 6$

$24 = 6 \times 4$

6	4
12	8
18	12
24	16
	20
	24

4

6 24

---

4 × 5 = 20

5 × 4 = 20

5	4
10	8
15	12
20	16
	20

5

4 20

$35 = 5 \times 7$

$35 = 7 \times 5$

7	5
14	10
21	15
28	20
35	25
	30
	35

7

5 35

---

5 × 6 = 30

6 × 5 = 30

6	5
12	10
18	15
24	20
30	25
	30

5

6 30

$25 = 5 \times 5$

5
10
15
20
25

5

5 25

---

4 × 9 = 36

9 × 4 = 36

9	4
18	8
27	12
36	16
	20
	24
	28
	32
	36

9

4 36

Home Multiplication Strategy Cards

5×8
8×5

5
$\times 9$ $\times 5$
   9

6×6

6 7
$\times 7$ $\times 6$

6×8
8×6

6 9
$\times 9$ $\times 6$

7×7

7 8
$\times 8$ $\times 7$

42 = 7 × 6

42 = 6 × 7

6	7
12	14
18	21
24	28
30	35
36	42
42	

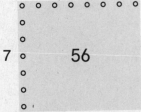

7

6 | 42

6
× 6
36

6
12
18
24
30

36

6

6 | 36

---

45 = 9 × 5

45 = 5 × 9

5	9
10	18
15	27
20	36
25	45
30	
35	
40	
45	

9

5 | 45

8	5
× 5	× 8
40	**40**

5	8
10	16
15	24
20	32
25	40
30	
35	
40	

5

8 | 40

---

56 = 7 × 8

56 = 8 × 7

8	7
16	14
24	21
32	28
40	35
48	42
56	49
	56

8

7 | 56

7
× 7
49

7
14
21
28
35

42
49

7

7 | 49

---

54 = 9 × 6

54 = 6 × 9

6	9
12	18
18	27
24	36
30	45
36	54
42	
48	
54	

9

6 | 54

6	8
× 8	× 6
48	**48**

6	8
12	16
18	24
24	32
30	40
36	48
42	
48	

8

6 | 48

Home Multiplication Strategy Cards

7×9
9×7

8
$\times\ 8$

9×8
8×9

9
$\times\ 9$

81 = 9 × 9

9
18
27
36
45

54
63
72
81

$$\begin{array}{r} 9 \\ \times\ 8 \\ \hline 72 \end{array} \qquad \begin{array}{r} 8 \\ \times\ 9 \\ \hline 72 \end{array}$$

8   9
16   18
24   27
32   36
40   45

48   54
56   63
64   72
72

64 = 8 × 8

8
16
24
32
40

48
56
64

$$\begin{array}{r} 7 \\ \times\ 9 \\ \hline 63 \end{array} \qquad \begin{array}{r} 9 \\ \times\ 7 \\ \hline 63 \end{array}$$

9   7
18   14
27   21
36   28
45   35

54   42
63   49
     56
     63

9 · 9 · 81

9 · 8 · 72

8 · 8 · 64

9 · 7 · 63

Home Multiplication Strategy Cards

$2\overline{)4}$

$4 \div 2$

$2\overline{)6}$

$6 \div 2$

$2\overline{)8}$

$8 \div 2$

$2\overline{)10}$

$10 \div 2$

$2\overline{)12}$

$12 \div 2$

$2\overline{)14}$

$14 \div 2$

$2\overline{)16}$

$16 \div 2$

$2\overline{)18}$

$18 \div 2$

$$5 \div 2)\overline{10} \qquad 2 \div 5)\overline{10}$$

2   5
4   10
6
8
10

5
2   o o o o o / 10

$$4 \div 2)\overline{8} \qquad 2 \div 4)\overline{8}$$

2   4
4   8
6
8

4
2   o o o o / 8

$$3 \div 2)\overline{6} \qquad 2 \div 3)\overline{6}$$

2   3
4   6
6

3
2   o o o / 6

$$2 \div 2)\overline{4}$$

2
4

2
2   o o / 4

$$9 \div 2)\overline{18} \qquad 2 \div 9)\overline{18}$$

2   9
4   18
6
8
10

12
14
16
18

9
2   o o o o o o o o o / 18

$$8 \div 2)\overline{16} \qquad 2 \div 8)\overline{16}$$

2   8
4   16
6
8
10

12
14
16

8
2   o o o o o o o o / 16

$$7 \div 2)\overline{14} \qquad 2 \div 7)\overline{14}$$

2   7
4   14
6
8
10

12
14

7
2   o o o o o o o / 14

$$6 \div 2)\overline{12} \qquad 2 \div 6)\overline{12}$$

2   6
4   12
6
8
10

12

6
2   o o o o o o / 12

Home Division Strategy Cards

$3\overline{)6}$

$6 \div 3$

$4\overline{)8}$

$8 \div 4$

$5\overline{)10}$

$10 \div 5$

$6\overline{)12}$

$12 \div 6$

$7\overline{)14}$

$14 \div 7$

$8\overline{)16}$

$16 \div 8$

$9\overline{)18}$

$18 \div 9$

$3\overline{)9}$

$9 \div 3$

Row 1

Card 1:

$$6\overline{)12}\ ^{2} \qquad 2\overline{)12}\ ^{6}$$

6   2
12   4
      6
      8
    10
    12

2
6 °12

Card 2:

$$5\overline{)10}\ ^{2} \qquad 2\overline{)10}\ ^{5}$$

5   2
10   4
      6
      8
    10

2
5 °10

Card 3:

$$4\overline{)8}\ ^{2} \qquad 2\overline{)8}\ ^{4}$$

4   2
8   4
      6
      8

2
4 °8

Card 4:

$$3\overline{)6}\ ^{2} \qquad 2\overline{)6}\ ^{3}$$

3   2
6   4
      6

2
3 °6

Row 2

Card 5:

$$3\overline{)9}\ ^{3}$$

3
6
9

3
3 °9

Card 6:

$$9\overline{)18}\ ^{2} \qquad 2\overline{)18}\ ^{9}$$

9   2
18   4
      6
      8
    10
    12
    14
    16
    18

2
9 °18

Card 7:

$$8\overline{)16}\ ^{2} \qquad 2\overline{)16}\ ^{8}$$

8   2
16   4
      6
      8
    10
    12
    14
    16

2
8 °16

Card 8:

$$7\overline{)14}\ ^{2} \qquad 2\overline{)14}\ ^{7}$$

7   2
14   4
      6
      8
    10
    12
    14

2
7 °14

Home Division Strategy Cards

$3\overline{)12}$
$12 \div 3$

$3\overline{)15}$
$15 \div 3$

$3\overline{)18}$
$18 \div 3$

$3\overline{)21}$
$21 \div 3$

$3\overline{)24}$
$24 \div 3$

$3\overline{)27}$
$27 \div 3$

$4\overline{)12}$
$12 \div 4$

$5\overline{)15}$
$15 \div 5$

7 **3**
3)21 7)21

3   7
6   14
9   21
12
15
18
21

7
3 | 21

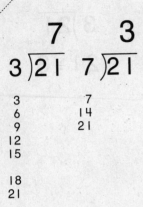

6 **3**
3)18 6)18

3   6
6   12
9   18
12
15
18

6
3 | 18

5 **3**
3)15 5)15

3   5
6   10
9   15
12
15

5
3 | 15

4 **3**
3)12 4)12

3   4
6   8
9   12
12

4
3 | 12

---

3 **5**
5)15 3)15

5   3
10   6
15   9
       12
       15

3
5 | 15

3 **4**
4)12 3)12

4   3
8   6
12   9
       12

3
4 | 12

9 **3**
3)27 9)27

3   9
6   18
9   27
12
15

18
21
24
27

9
3 | 27

8 **3**
3)24 8)24

3   8
6   16
9   24
12
15

18
21
24

8
3 | 24

Home Division Strategy Cards

$6\overline{)18}$
$18 \div 6$

$7\overline{)21}$
$21 \div 7$

$8\overline{)24}$
$24 \div 8$

$9\overline{)27}$
$27 \div 9$

$4\overline{)16}$
$16 \div 4$

$4\overline{)20}$
$20 \div 4$

$4\overline{)24}$
$24 \div 4$

$4\overline{)28}$
$28 \div 4$

Row 1

3
9)27
9
18
27

9
3)27
3
6
9
12
15

18
21
24
27

3
9 ○ 27

3
8)24
8
16
24

8
3)24
3
6
9
12
15

18
21
24

3
8 ○ 24

3
7)21
7
14
21

7
3)21
3
6
9
12
15

18
21

3
7 ○ 21

3
6)18
6
12
18

6
3)18
3
6
9
12
15

18

3
6 ○ 18

Row 2

7
4)28
4
8
12
16
20

24
28

4
7)28
7
14
21
28

7
4 ○ 28

6
4)24
4
8
12
16
20

24

4
6)24
6
12
18
24

6
4 ○ 24

5
4)20
4
8
12
16
20

4
5)20
5
10
15
20

5
4 ○ 20

4
4)16
4
8
12
16

4
4 ○ 16

Home Division Strategy Cards

$4\overline{)32}$

$32 \div 4$

$4\overline{)36}$

$36 \div 4$

$5\overline{)20}$

$20 \div 5$

$6\overline{)24}$

$24 \div 6$

$7\overline{)28}$

$28 \div 7$

$8\overline{)32}$

$32 \div 8$

$9\overline{)36}$

$36 \div 9$

$5\overline{)25}$

$25 \div 5$

4 6
$6\overline{)24}$ $4\overline{)24}$

6	4
12	8
18	12
24	16
	20
	24

4
6 24

4 5
$5\overline{)20}$ $4\overline{)20}$

5	4
10	8
15	12
20	16
	20

4
5 20

9 4
$4\overline{)36}$ $9\overline{)36}$

4	9
8	18
12	27
16	36
20	
24	
28	
32	
36	

9
4 36

8 4
$4\overline{)32}$ $8\overline{)32}$

4	8
8	16
12	24
16	32
20	
24	
28	
32	

8
4 32

5
$5\overline{)25}$

5
10
15
20
25

5
5 25

4 9
$9\overline{)36}$ $4\overline{)36}$

9	4
18	8
27	12
36	16
	20
	24
	28
	32
	36

4
9 36

4 8
$8\overline{)32}$ $4\overline{)32}$

8	4
16	8
24	12
32	16
	20
	24
	28
	32

4
8 32

4 7
$7\overline{)28}$ $4\overline{)28}$

7	4
14	8
21	12
28	16
	20
	24
	28

4
7 28

Home Division Strategy Cards

$5 \overline{)30}$

$30 \div 5$

$5 \overline{)35}$

$35 \div 5$

$5 \overline{)40}$

$40 \div 5$

$5 \overline{)45}$

$45 \div 5$

$6 \overline{)30}$

$30 \div 6$

$7 \overline{)35}$

$35 \div 7$

$8 \overline{)40}$

$40 \div 8$

$9 \overline{)45}$

$45 \div 9$

Top Row

9 | 5

5)45 9)45

5	9
10	18
15	27
20	36
25	45
30	
35	
40	
45	

9
5) 45

8 | 5

5)40 8)40

5	8
10	16
15	24
20	32
25	40
30	
35	
40	

8
5) 40

7 | 5

5)35 7)35

5	7
10	14
15	21
20	28
25	35
30	
35	

7
5) 35

6 | 5

5)30 6)30

5	6
10	12
15	18
20	24
25	30
30	

6
5) 30

Bottom Row

5 | 9

9)45 5)45

9	5
18	10
27	15
36	20
45	25
	30
	35
	40
	45

5
9) 45

5 | 8

8)40 5)40

8	5
16	10
24	15
32	20
40	25
	30
	35
	40

5
8) 40

5 | 7

7)35 5)35

7	5
14	10
21	15
28	20
35	25
	30
	35

5
7) 35

5 | 6

6)30 5)30

6	5
12	10
18	15
24	20
30	25
	30

5
6) 30

Home Division Strategy Cards

$6\overline{)36}$

$36 \div 6$

$6\overline{)42}$

$42 \div 6$

$6\overline{)48}$

$48 \div 6$

$6\overline{)54}$

$54 \div 6$

$7\overline{)42}$

$42 \div 7$

$8\overline{)48}$

$48 \div 8$

$9\overline{)54}$

$54 \div 9$

$7\overline{)49}$

$49 \div 7$

Card 1

9
6)54

6
9)54

6	9
12	18
18	27
24	36
30	45
36	54
42	
48	
54	

9
6 · 54

Card 2

8
6)48

6
8)48

6	8
12	16
18	24
24	32
30	40
36	48
42	
48	

8
6 · 48

Card 3

7
6)42

6
7)42

6	7
12	14
18	21
24	28
30	35
36	42
42	

7
6 · 42

Card 4

6
6)36

6
12
18
24
30

36

6
6 · 36

Card 5

7
7)49

7
14
21
28
35

42
49

7
7 · 49

Card 6

6
9)54

9
6)54

9	6
18	12
27	18
36	24
45	30
54	36
	42
	48
	54

6
9 · 54

Card 7

6
8)48

8
6)48

8	6
16	12
24	18
32	24
40	30
48	36
	42
	48

6
8 · 48

Card 8

6
7)42

7
6)42

7	6
14	12
21	18
28	24
35	30
42	36
	42

6
7 · 42

Home Division Strategy Cards

$7 \overline{)56}$

$56 \div 7$

$7 \overline{)63}$

$63 \div 7$

$8 \overline{)56}$

$56 \div 8$

$9 \overline{)63}$

$63 \div 9$

$8 \overline{)64}$

$64 \div 8$

$8 \overline{)72}$

$72 \div 8$

$9 \overline{)72}$

$72 \div 9$

$9 \overline{)81}$

$81 \div 9$

Top row

7	9
9)63	7)63

9	7
18	14
27	21
36	28
45	35
54	42
63	49
	56
	63

7
9 · · · · · · · 63

7	8
8)56	7)56

8	7
16	14
24	21
32	28
40	35
48	42
56	49
	56

7
8 · · · · · · · 56

9	7
7)63	9)63

7	9
14	18
21	27
28	36
35	45
42	54
49	63
56	
63	

9
7 · · · · · · · 63

8	7
7)56	8)56

7	8
14	16
21	24
28	32
35	40
42	48
49	56
56	

8
7 · · · · · · · 56

Bottom row

9
9)81

9
18
27
36
45
54
63
72
81

9
9 · · · · · · · 81

8	9
9)72	8)72

9	8
18	16
27	24
36	32
45	40
54	48
63	56
72	64
	72

8
9 · · · · · · · 72

9	8
8)72	9)72

8	9
16	18
24	27
32	36
40	45
48	54
56	63
64	72
72	

9
8 · · · · · · · 72

8
8)64

8
16
24
32
40
48
56
64

8
8 · · · · · · · 64

© Houghton Mifflin Harcourt Publishing Company

Home Division Strategy Cards

Homework

Name _____ Date _____

© Houghton Mifflin Harcourt Publishing Company

Home Study Sheet B

4s

Count-bys	Mixed Up ×	Mixed Up ÷
1 × 4 = 4	4 × 4 = 16	12 ÷ 4 = 3
2 × 4 = 8	1 × 4 = 4	36 ÷ 4 = 9
3 × 4 = 12	7 × 4 = 28	24 ÷ 4 = 6
4 × 4 = 16	3 × 4 = 12	4 ÷ 4 = 1
5 × 4 = 20	9 × 4 = 36	20 ÷ 4 = 5
6 × 4 = 24	10 × 4 = 40	28 ÷ 4 = 7
7 × 4 = 28	2 × 4 = 8	8 ÷ 4 = 2
8 × 4 = 32	5 × 4 = 20	40 ÷ 4 = 10
9 × 4 = 36	8 × 4 = 32	32 ÷ 4 = 8
10 × 4 = 40	6 × 4 = 24	16 ÷ 4 = 4

1s

Count-bys	Mixed Up ×	Mixed Up ÷
1 × 1 = 1	5 × 1 = 5	10 ÷ 1 = 10
2 × 1 = 2	7 × 1 = 7	8 ÷ 1 = 8
3 × 1 = 3	10 × 1 = 10	4 ÷ 1 = 4
4 × 1 = 4	1 × 1 = 1	9 ÷ 1 = 9
5 × 1 = 5	8 × 1 = 8	6 ÷ 1 = 6
6 × 1 = 6	4 × 1 = 4	7 ÷ 1 = 7
7 × 1 = 7	9 × 1 = 9	1 ÷ 1 = 1
8 × 1 = 8	3 × 1 = 3	2 ÷ 1 = 2
9 × 1 = 9	2 × 1 = 2	5 ÷ 1 = 5
10 × 1 = 10	6 × 1 = 6	3 ÷ 1 = 3

3s

Count-bys	Mixed Up ×	Mixed Up ÷
1 × 3 = 3	5 × 3 = 15	27 ÷ 3 = 9
2 × 3 = 6	1 × 3 = 3	6 ÷ 3 = 2
3 × 3 = 9	8 × 3 = 24	18 ÷ 3 = 6
4 × 3 = 12	10 × 3 = 30	30 ÷ 3 = 10
5 × 3 = 15	3 × 3 = 9	9 ÷ 3 = 3
6 × 3 = 18	7 × 3 = 21	3 ÷ 3 = 1
7 × 3 = 21	9 × 3 = 27	12 ÷ 3 = 4
8 × 3 = 24	2 × 3 = 6	24 ÷ 3 = 8
9 × 3 = 27	4 × 3 = 12	15 ÷ 3 = 5
10 × 3 = 30	6 × 3 = 18	21 ÷ 3 = 7

0s

Count-bys	Mixed Up ×
1 × 0 = 0	3 × 0 = 0
2 × 0 = 0	10 × 0 = 0
3 × 0 = 0	5 × 0 = 0
4 × 0 = 0	8 × 0 = 0
5 × 0 = 0	7 × 0 = 0
6 × 0 = 0	2 × 0 = 0
7 × 0 = 0	9 × 0 = 0
8 × 0 = 0	6 × 0 = 0
9 × 0 = 0	1 × 0 = 0
10 × 0 = 0	4 × 0 = 0

Homework

Multiply or divide to find the unknown numbers. Then check your answers at the bottom of the page.

1. $3 \times 5 =$ ☐

2. $27 \div 9 =$ ☐

3. $2\overline{)20}$ ☐

4. $7 \cdot 9 =$ ☐

5. $2 *$ ☐ $= 12$

6. $18 / 3 =$ ☐

7. $9 \times 5 =$ ☐

8. $3 *$ ☐ $= 21$

9. $\frac{81}{9} =$ ☐

10. $6 \div 3 =$ ☐

11. $8 \times 2 =$ ☐

12. $\frac{14}{2} =$ ☐

13. $3 \cdot 3 =$ ☐

14. ☐ $* 9 = 72$

15. $90 \div 9 =$ ☐

16. ☐ $* 2 = 18$

17. $24 \div$ ☐ $= 8$

18. $12 /$ ☐ $= 6$

19. $6 \cdot 5 =$ ☐

20. $4 \times$ ☐ $= 40$

21. ☐ $\cdot 9 = 54$

1. 15 **2.** 3 **3.** 10 **4.** 63 **5.** 6 **6.** 6 **7.** 45 **8.** 7 **9.** 9 **10.** 2 **11.** 16
12. 7 **13.** 9 **14.** 8 **15.** 10 **16.** 9 **17.** 3 **18.** 2 **19.** 30 **20.** 10 **21.** 6

Multiplication and Area

Homework

Use this table to practice your 4s count-bys, multiplications, and divisions. Then have your Homework Helper test you.

4s	× In Order	× Mixed Up	÷ Mixed Up
	$1 \times 4 = 4$	$9 \times 4 = 36$	$20 \div 4 = 5$
	$2 \times 4 = 8$	$5 \times 4 = 20$	$4 \div 4 = 1$
	$3 \times 4 = 12$	$7 \times 4 = 28$	$16 \div 4 = 4$
	$4 \times 4 = 16$	$2 \times 4 = 8$	$36 \div 4 = 9$
	$5 \times 4 = 20$	$4 \times 4 = 16$	$24 \div 4 = 6$
	$6 \times 4 = 24$	$1 \times 4 = 4$	$12 \div 4 = 3$
	$7 \times 4 = 28$	$6 \times 4 = 24$	$32 \div 4 = 8$
	$8 \times 4 = 32$	$8 \times 4 = 32$	$8 \div 4 = 2$
	$9 \times 4 = 36$	$3 \times 4 = 12$	$40 \div 4 = 10$
	$10 \times 4 = 40$	$10 \times 4 = 40$	$28 \div 4 = 7$

Multiply and Divide with 4 **71**

Homework

Multiply or divide to find the unknown numbers. Then check your answers at the bottom of this page.

1. $4 \times 9 = \boxed{}$

2. $12 \div 3 = \boxed{}$

3. $4 * 8 = \boxed{}$

4. $30 / 3 = \boxed{}$

5. $3 \cdot \boxed{} = 24$

6. $9\overline{)81}^{\,\boxed{}}$

7. $6 \times 3 = \boxed{}$

8. $\dfrac{27}{3} = \boxed{}$

9. $9 \times 10 = \boxed{}$

10. $24 / 4 = \boxed{}$

11. $10 \cdot 3 = \boxed{}$

12. $16 \div 4 = \boxed{}$

13. $9 * \boxed{} = 63$

14. $\dfrac{36}{4} = \boxed{}$

15. $7 \cdot 4 = \boxed{}$

16. $20 / 4 = \boxed{}$

17. $9\overline{)54}^{\,\boxed{}}$

18. $3 * 7 = \boxed{}$

19. $\boxed{} \times 4 = 4$

20. $15 \div 3 = \boxed{}$

21. $4 \times \boxed{} = 16$

1. 36 2. 4 3. 32 4. 10 5. 8 6. 9 7. 18 8. 9 9. 90 10. 6 11. 30
12. 4 13. 7 14. 9 15. 28 16. 5 17. 6 18. 21 19. 1 20. 5 21. 4

Multiply and Divide with 4

Home Check Sheet 4: 3s and 4s

3s Multiplication	3s Divisions	4s Multiplications	4s Divisions
8 × 3 = 24	9 / 3 = 3	1 × 4 = 4	40 / 4 = 10
3 • 2 = 6	21 ÷ 3 = 7	4 • 5 = 20	12 ÷ 4 = 3
3 * 5 = 15	27 / 3 = 9	8 * 4 = 32	24 / 4 = 6
10 × 3 = 30	3 ÷ 3 = 1	3 × 4 = 12	8 ÷ 4 = 2
3 • 3 = 9	18 / 3 = 6	4 • 6 = 24	4 / 4 = 1
3 * 6 = 18	12 ÷ 3 = 4	4 * 9 = 36	28 ÷ 4 = 7
7 × 3 = 21	30 / 3 = 10	10 × 4 = 40	32 / 4 = 8
3 • 9 = 27	6 ÷ 3 = 2	4 • 7 = 28	16 ÷ 4 = 4
4 * 3 = 12	24 / 3 = 8	4 * 4 = 16	36 / 4 = 9
3 × 1 = 3	15 / 3 = 5	2 × 4 = 8	20 / 4 = 5
3 • 4 = 12	21 ÷ 3 = 7	4 • 3 = 12	4 ÷ 4 = 1
3 * 3 = 9	3 / 3 = 1	4 * 2 = 8	32 / 4 = 8
3 × 10 = 30	9 ÷ 3 = 3	9 × 4 = 36	8 ÷ 4 = 2
2 • 3 = 6	27 / 3 = 9	1 • 4 = 4	16 / 4 = 4
3 * 7 = 21	30 ÷ 3 = 10	4 * 6 = 24	36 ÷ 4 = 9
6 × 3 = 18	18 / 3 = 6	5 × 4 = 20	12 / 4 = 3
5 • 3 = 15	6 ÷ 3 = 2	4 • 4 = 16	40 ÷ 4 = 10
3 * 8 = 24	15 ÷ 3 = 5	7 * 4 = 28	20 ÷ 4 = 5
9 × 3 = 27	12 / 3 = 4	8 × 4 = 32	24 / 4 = 6
2 • 3 = 6	24 ÷ 3 = 8	10 • 4 = 40	28 ÷ 4 = 7

Homework

Study Plan

Homework Helper

Solve each problem.

1. Colin had 16 puzzles. He gave 4 puzzles to each of his nephews. How many nephews does Colin have?

_____

2. Allegra listed the names of her classmates in 4 columns, with 7 names in each column. How many classmates does Allegra have?

_____

> This large rectangle is made up of two small rectangles.

3. Find the area of the large rectangle by finding the areas of the two small rectangles and adding them.

_____

4. Find the area of the large rectangle by multiplying the number of rows by the number of square units in each row.

_____

> This Equal-Shares drawing shows that 6 groups of 9 is the same as 5 groups of 9 plus 1 group of 9.

5. Find 5 × ⑨ and 1 × ⑨, and add the answers.

_____

6. Find 6 × ⑨ Did you get the same answer as in question 5?

_____

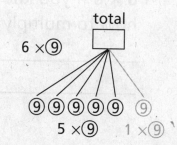

Remembering

Multiply or divide to find the unknown numbers.

1. $18 \div 2 = \boxed{}$ **2.** $9 * \boxed{} = 72$ **3.** $\frac{40}{5} = \boxed{}$

4. $2 \bullet 7 = \boxed{}$ **5.** $5\overline{)30}$ with $\boxed{}$ on top   **6.** $\boxed{} \times 10 = 70$

Write an equation and solve the problem.

7. Sydney has piles of 10 sticker sheets. She has
100 sheets in all. How many piles does she have?

_____

8. Mr. Thomas gives 4 crayons to each of 8 students.
How many crayons does he give out?

_____

**Make a rectangle drawing to represent each multiplication.
Then find the product.**

9. $3 \bullet 8 = \boxed{}$ **10.** $2 \bullet 9 = \boxed{}$

11. Stretch Your Thinking Explain how you can solve
8×8 if you know how to multiply with 4 but not
how to multiply with 8.

_____

_____

Multiply and Divide with 4

Homework

Study Plan

_____

Homework Helper

Write an equation and solve the problem.

1. Pablo hung his watercolor paintings in an array with 3 rows and 4 columns. How many paintings did Pablo hang?

   _____

2. A group of 7 friends went on a hiking trip. Each person took 3 granola bars. What total number of granola bars did the friends take?

   _____

3. Jon had 45 sheets of construction paper. He used 9 sheets to make paper snowflakes. How many sheets does he have now?

   _____

You can combine multiplications you know to find multiplications you don't know.

4. Find this product: $5 \times 8 =$ _____

5. Find this product: $1 \times 8 =$ _____

6. Use the answers to Exercises 4 and 5

   to find this product: $6 \times 8 =$ _____

Name _____ **Date** _____

Remembering

Write an equation and solve the problem.

1. Tamara has 3 soccer practices each week. How many practices will she have after 7 weeks?

2. David has 24 items to put in bags. If he puts 3 items in each bag, how many bags does he need?

_____   _____

Solve each problem.

The Equal Shares drawing at the right shows that 8 groups of 4 is the same as 7 groups of 4 plus 1 group of 4.

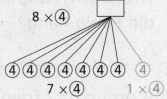

3. Find $7 \times \textcircled{4}$ and $1 \times (\ \cdot\ )$. Then add the answers.

_____

4. Find $8 \times \textcircled{4}$. Did you get the same answer as in exercise 3?

_____

5. Find the area of the large rectangle by finding the area of the two small rectangles and adding them.

_____

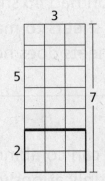

6. Find the area of the large rectangle by multiplying the number of rows by the number of squares in each row.

_____

7. **Stretch Your Thinking** Select a _____ card. Without looking at the back, wr_____ _____ategies you can use to solve it. Turn it over_____.

_____
_____

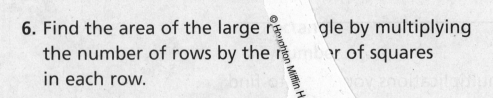

Use the Strategy Cards

Homework

	× In Order	× Mixed Up	÷ Mixed Up
1s	$1 \times 1 = 1$	$3 \times 1 = 3$	$7 \div 1 = 7$
	$2 \times 1 = 2$	$7 \times 1 = 7$	$10 \div 1 = 10$
	$3 \times 1 = 3$	$1 \times 1 = 1$	$3 \div 1 = 3$
	$4 \times 1 = 4$	$10 \times 1 = 10$	$9 \div 1 = 9$
	$5 \times 1 = 5$	$6 \times 1 = 6$	$1 \div 1 = 1$
	$6 \times 1 = 6$	$2 \times 1 = 2$	$4 \div 1 = 4$
	$7 \times 1 = 7$	$5 \times 1 = 5$	$5 \div 1 = 5$
	$8 \times 1 = 8$	$8 \times 1 = 8$	$8 \div 1 = 8$
	$9 \times 1 = 9$	$4 \times 1 = 4$	$2 \div 1 = 2$
	$10 \times 1 = 10$	$9 \times 1 = 9$	$6 \div 1 = 6$

	× In Order	× Mixed Up
0s	$1 \times 0 = 0$	$3 \times 0 = 0$
	$2 \times 0 = 0$	$7 \times 0 = 0$
	$3 \times 0 = 0$	$1 \times 0 = 0$
	$4 \times 0 = 0$	$10 \times 0 = 0$
	$5 \times 0 = 0$	$6 \times 0 = 0$
	$6 \times 0 = 0$	$2 \times 0 = 0$
	$7 \times 0 = 0$	$5 \times 0 = 0$
	$8 \times 0 = 0$	$8 \times 0 = 0$
	$9 \times 0 = 0$	$4 \times 0 = 0$
	$10 \times 0 = 0$	$9 \times 0 = 0$

Multiply and Divide with 1 and 0 **81**

Homework

Name _____ **Date** _____

Multiply or divide to find the unknown numbers.
Then check your answers at the bottom of this page.

1. $4 \times 1 = \boxed{}$

2. $12 \div 3 = \boxed{}$

3. $7 * 0 = \boxed{}$

4. $0 / 5 = \boxed{}$

5. $4 \cdot \boxed{} = 8$

6. $\frac{2}{1} = \boxed{}$

7. $10 \times 1 = \boxed{}$

8. $\frac{0}{4} = \boxed{}$

9. $1 \times 0 = \boxed{}$

10. $3\overline{)9}$

11. $10 \cdot 9 = \boxed{}$

12. $0 \div 1 = \boxed{}$

13. $3 * \boxed{} = 3$

14. $\frac{8}{1} = \boxed{}$

15. $0 \cdot 7 = \boxed{}$

16. $24 / 3 = \boxed{}$

17. $1 \div 1 = \boxed{}$

18. $10 * 2 = \boxed{}$

19. $\boxed{} \times 3 = 0$

20. $3\overline{)18}$

21. $1 \times \boxed{} = 4$

22. $\boxed{} \times 5 = $

23. $6 \cdot 9 = \boxed{}$

24. $10 \div 1 = \boxed{}$

23. 54 **24.** 10

13. 1 **14.** 8 **15.** 0 **16.** 8 **17.** 1 **18.** 20 **19.** 0 **20.**

1. 4 **2.** 4 **3.** 0 **4.** 0 **5.** 2 **6.** 2 **7.** 10 **8.** 0 **9.** 0

Homework

Study Plan

_____

Homework Helper

Complete.

1. $3 \times (4 \times 2) = \boxed{}$ **2.** $(5 \times 2) \times 8 = \boxed{}$ **3.** $5 \times (0 \times 9) = \boxed{}$

4. $25 \times 1 = \boxed{}$ **5.** $3 \times 9 = 9 \times = \boxed{} = \boxed{}$ **6.** $6 \times (3 \times 2) = \boxed{}$

Write an equation and solve the problem.

7. Paul put birthday candles on his brother's cake. He arranged them in an array with 8 rows and 1 column. How many candles did he put on the cake? _____

8. There are 24 people in the brass section of the marching band. They stood in an array with 4 people in each row. How many rows were there?

_____

9. Freya doesn't like peppers, so she grew 0 peppers in her garden. She divided the peppers equally among her 4 cousins. How many peppers did each cousin get? _____

10. Cal had 6 comic books. After he gave 1 comic book to each of his cousins, he had none left. How many cousins does Cal have?

_____

Multiply and Divide with 1 and 0 **83**

Remembering

Solve each problem.

1. Find the area of the large rectangle by finding the area of the two small rectangles and adding them.

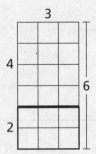

_____

2. Find the area of the large rectangle by multiplying the number of rows by the number of squares units in each row.

_____

Write an equation and solve the problem.

3. Dwight has 72 pennies in a jar. He takes out 9 pennies. How many pennies are in the jar now?

_____

4. There are 3 soccer bags. Each bag has 7 soccer balls. How many soccer balls are there in all?

_____

Multiply or divide to find the unknown numbers.

5. $3\overline{)21}$

6. $\boxed{} * 10 = 80$

7. $\dfrac{81}{9} = \boxed{}$

8. $9 \times \boxed{} = 63$

9. $2 \cdot 6 = \boxed{}$

10. $\boxed{} \div 5 = 5$

11. **Stretch Your Thinking** Write and solve an equation with the numbers 0 and 9. Then write an equation with the numbers 1 and 9 that has the same answer.

_____

Multiply and Divide with 1 and 0

Study Plan
Homework Helper

**Read each problem and decide what type of problem it is.
Write the letter from the list below. Then write an equation
and solve the problem.**

a. Array Multiplication

b. Array Division

c. Equal Groups Multiplication

d. Equal Groups Division with an Unknown Group Size

e. Equal Groups Division with an Unknown Multiplier
(number of groups)

1. A farmer collected eggs from the henhouse. He can put 36 eggs in a carton. A carton will hold 6 eggs in a row. How many rows does the egg carton have?

_____

2. The Watertown science contest allowed teams of 5 students to compete. If 45 students entered the contest, how many teams competed?

_____

3. The Happy Feet Shoe Store is having a sale. 10 pairs of shoes are displayed on each row of the sale rack. If the rack has 8 rows, how many pairs of shoes are on sale?

_____

4. Una has 5 goldfish. She bought 2 small water plants for each goldfish. How many plants did she buy?

_____

5. Yolanda made 16 barrettes. She divided the barrettes equally among her 4 friends. How many barrettes did each friend get?

_____

6. Carson has 12 baseball cards to give away. If he gives 3 cards to each friend, how many friends can he give cards to?

_____

Remembering

You can combine multiplications you know to find multiplications you don't know.

1. Find this product: $3 \times 7 =$ _____

2. Find this product: $4 \times 7 =$ _____

3. Use the answers to Exercises 1 and 2 to find this product: $7 \times 7 =$ _____

Write an equation and solve the problem.

Show your work.

4. Susan buys 9 packages of cups. There are 8 cups in each package. How many cups does she buy altogether?

_____

5. The football team has 30 players. The players line up to exercise with 5 in each row. How many rows are there?

_____

6. Bill scored 63 points on his video game. He gets 9 points for each level he completes. How many levels did he complete?

_____

Complete.

7. $4 \times (5 \times 1) = \boxed{}$ **8.** $6 \times 9 = 9 \times \boxed{} = \boxed{}$ **9.** $(10 \times 1) \times 7 = \boxed{}$

10. $9 \times (5 \times 0) = \boxed{}$ **11.** $26 \times 1 = \boxed{}$ **12.** $5 \times (3 \times 3) = \boxed{}$

13. **Stretch Your Thinking** Write a word problem using $24 \div 3$. Then solve your problem.

_____

_____

     Solve and Create Word Problems

Homework

Home Check Sheet 5: 1s and 0s

1s Multiplications	1s Divisions	0s Multiplications
$1 \times 4 = 4$	$10 / 1 = 10$	$4 \times 0 = 0$
$5 \cdot 1 = 5$	$5 \div 1 = 5$	$2 \cdot 0 = 0$
$7 * 1 = 7$	$7 / 1 = 7$	$0 * 8 = 0$
$1 \times 8 = 8$	$9 \div 1 = 9$	$0 \times 5 = 0$
$1 \cdot 6 = 6$	$3 / 1 = 3$	$6 \cdot 0 = 0$
$10 * 1 = 10$	$10 \div 1 = 10$	$0 * 7 = 0$
$1 \times 9 = 9$	$2 / 1 = 2$	$0 \times 2 = 0$
$3 \cdot 1 = 3$	$8 \div 1 = 8$	$0 \cdot 9 = 0$
$1 * 2 = 2$	$6 / 1 = 6$	$10 * 0 = 0$
$1 \times 1 = 1$	$9 / 1 = 9$	$1 \times 0 = 0$
$8 \cdot 1 = 8$	$1 \div 1 = 1$	$0 \cdot 6 = 0$
$1 * 7 = 7$	$5 / 1 = 5$	$9 * 0 = 0$
$1 \times 5 = 5$	$3 \div 1 = 3$	$0 \times 4 = 0$
$6 \cdot 1 = 6$	$4 / 1 = 4$	$3 \cdot 0 = 0$
$1 * 1 = 1$	$2 \div 1 = 2$	$0 * 3 = 0$
$1 \times 10 = 10$	$8 / 1 = 8$	$8 \times 0 = 0$
$9 \cdot 1 = 9$	$4 \div 1 = 4$	$0 \cdot 10 = 0$
$4 * 1 = 4$	$7 \div 1 = 7$	$0 * 1 = 0$
$2 \times 1 = 2$	$1 / 1 = 1$	$5 \times 0 = 0$
$1 \cdot 3 = 3$	$6 \div 1 = 6$	$7 \cdot 0 = 0$

Homework

Home Check Sheet 6: Mixed 3s, 4s, 0s, and 1s

3s, 4s, 0s, 1s Multiplications	3s, 4s, 0s, 1s Multiplications	3s, 4s, 1s Divisions	3s, 4s, 1s Divisions
$5 \times 3 = 15$	$0 \times 5 = 0$	$18 / 3 = 6$	$4 / 1 = 4$
$6 \cdot 4 = 24$	$10 \cdot 1 = 10$	$20 \div 4 = 5$	$21 \div 3 = 7$
$9 * 0 = 0$	$6 * 3 = 18$	$1 / 1 = 1$	$16 / 4 = 4$
$7 \times 1 = 7$	$2 \times 4 = 8$	$21 \div 3 = 7$	$9 \div 1 = 9$
$3 \cdot 3 = 9$	$5 \cdot 0 = 0$	$12 / 4 = 3$	$15 / 3 = 5$
$4 * 7 = 28$	$1 * 2 = 2$	$5 \div 1 = 5$	$8 \div 4 = 2$
$0 \times 10 = 0$	$10 \times 3 = 30$	$15 / 3 = 5$	$5 / 1 = 5$
$1 \cdot 6 = 6$	$5 \cdot 4 = 20$	$24 \div 4 = 6$	$30 \div 3 = 10$
$3 * 4 = 12$	$0 * 8 = 0$	$7 / 1 = 7$	$12 / 4 = 3$
$5 \times 4 = 20$	$6 \times 3 = 18$	$12 / 3 = 4$	$8 / 1 = 8$
$0 \cdot 5 = 0$	$10 \cdot 3 = 30$	$36 \div 4 = 9$	$27 \div 3 = 9$
$9 * 1 = 9$	$9 * 4 = 36$	$6 / 1 = 6$	$40 / 4 = 10$
$2 \times 3 = 6$	$1 \times 0 = 0$	$12 \div 3 = 4$	$4 \div 1 = 4$
$3 \cdot 4 = 12$	$1 \cdot 6 = 6$	$16 / 4 = 4$	$9 / 3 = 3$
$0 * 9 = 0$	$3 * 6 = 18$	$7 \div 1 = 7$	$16 \div 4 = 4$
$1 \times 5 = 5$	$7 \times 4 = 28$	$9 / 3 = 3$	$10 / 1 = 10$
$2 \cdot 3 = 6$	$6 \cdot 0 = 0$	$8 \div 4 = 2$	$9 \div 3 = 3$
$4 * 4 = 16$	$8 * 1 = 8$	$2 \div 1 = 2$	$20 \div 4 = 5$
$9 \times 0 = 0$	$3 \times 9 = 27$	$6 / 3 = 2$	$6 / 1 = 6$
$1 \cdot 1 = 1$	$1 \cdot 4 = 4$	$32 \div 4 = 8$	$24 \div 3 = 8$

Home Check Sheet 6: Mixed 3s, 4s, 0s, and 1s

Homework

Find the number.

1. I am 5 more than 6 times 10. What number am I? _____

2. I am 3 less than 8 times 4. What number am I? _____

3. 7 times a number is 21. What is the number? _____

4. 9 times a number is 18. What is the number? _____

5. Use the chart to complete the pictograph.

What is your hobby?

Hobby	Number of Students
Coin Collecting	12
Playing Sports	36
Playing Music	20
Taking Care of Pets	24

Hobbies

Coin Collecting	
Playing Sports	
Playing Music	
Taking Care of Pets	

Each ▮ = 4 third graders

Remembering

Read each problem and decide what type of problem it is. Write the letter from the list below. Then write an equation and solve the problem.

a. Array Multiplication
b. Array Division
c. Equal Groups of Multiplication
d. Equal Groups Division with Unknown Group Size
e. Equal Groups Division with an Unknown Multiplier (number of groups)

1. There are 40 toys in 5 boxes. Each box has the same number of toys. How many toys are in each box?

2. Sangeeta has two dogs. She buys 2 collars for each of her dogs. How many collars does she buy?

Write an equation and solve the problem.

Show your work.

3. Darci puts 15 tulips in 5 vases. If she puts the same number of tulips in each vase, how many tulips will be in each vase?

4. Miss Lin has 5 baskets. She puts 4 pears in each basket. How many pears are in the baskets?

5. Steven receives an order for 80 flash drives. He puts the same number of flash drives in 10 boxes. How many flash drives are in each box?

6. **Stretch Your Thinking** Solve the riddle. I am 6 more than 2 times 9. What number am I? Now make up your own riddle for the number 68.

Focus on Mathematical Practices

Homework

Use this chart to practice your 6s count-bys, multiplications, and divisions. Then have your Homework Helper test you.

	× In Order	× Mixed Up	÷ Mixed Up
6s	$1 \times 6 = 6$	$2 \times 6 = 12$	$18 \div 6 = 3$
	$2 \times 6 = 12$	$8 \times 6 = 48$	$60 \div 6 = 10$
	$3 \times 6 = 18$	$5 \times 6 = 30$	$30 \div 6 = 5$
	$4 \times 6 = 24$	$9 \times 6 = 54$	$48 \div 6 = 8$
	$5 \times 6 = 30$	$1 \times 6 = 6$	$12 \div 6 = 2$
	$6 \times 6 = 36$	$7 \times 6 = 42$	$6 \div 6 = 1$
	$7 \times 6 = 42$	$4 \times 6 = 24$	$36 \div 6 = 6$
	$8 \times 6 = 48$	$3 \times 6 = 18$	$24 \div 6 = 4$
	$9 \times 6 = 54$	$10 \times 6 = 60$	$54 \div 6 = 9$
	$10 \times 6 = 60$	$6 \times 6 = 36$	$42 \div 6 = 7$

Homework

Multiply or divide to find the unknown numbers.
Then check your answers at the bottom of this page.

1. $5 \times 5 = \boxed{}$

2. $12 \div 6 = \boxed{}$

3. $7 * 4 = \boxed{}$

4. $42 / 6 = \boxed{}$

5. $6 \cdot \boxed{} = 48$

6. $\frac{6}{1} = \boxed{}$

7. $10 \times 6 = \boxed{}$

8. $9\overline{)27}$ with $\boxed{}$

9. $6 \times 0 = \boxed{}$

10. $20 / 4 = \boxed{}$

11. $6 \cdot 6 = \boxed{}$

12. $18 \div 3 = \boxed{}$

13. $9 * \boxed{} = 54$

14. $\frac{60}{6} = \boxed{}$

15. $2 \cdot 7 = \boxed{}$

16. $16 / 4 = \boxed{}$

17. $6 \div 6 = \boxed{}$

18. $6 * 7 = \boxed{}$

19. $\boxed{} \times 7 = 0$

20. $9\overline{)45}$ with $\boxed{}$

21. $1 \times \boxed{} = 10$

1. 25 2. 2 3. 28 4. 7 5. 8 6. 6 7. 60 8. 3 9. 0 10. 5 11. 36 12. 6 13. 6 14. 10 15. 14 16. 4 17. 1 18. 42 19. 0 20. 5 21. 10

Multiply and Divide with 6

Homework

Name	Date

Home Study Sheet C

6s

Count-bys	Mixed Up ×	Mixed Up ÷
1 × 6 = 6	10 × 6 = 60	54 ÷ 6 = 9
2 × 6 = 12	8 × 6 = 48	30 ÷ 6 = 5
3 × 6 = 18	2 × 6 = 12	12 ÷ 6 = 2
4 × 6 = 24	6 × 6 = 36	60 ÷ 6 = 10
5 × 6 = 30	4 × 6 = 24	48 ÷ 6 = 8
6 × 6 = 36	1 × 6 = 6	36 ÷ 6 = 6
7 × 6 = 42	9 × 6 = 54	6 ÷ 6 = 1
8 × 6 = 48	3 × 6 = 18	42 ÷ 6 = 7
9 × 6 = 54	7 × 6 = 42	18 ÷ 6 = 3
10 × 6 = 60	5 × 6 = 30	24 ÷ 6 = 4

7s

Count-bys	Mixed Up ×	Mixed Up ÷
1 × 7 = 7	6 × 7 = 42	70 ÷ 7 = 10
2 × 7 = 14	8 × 7 = 56	14 ÷ 7 = 2
3 × 7 = 21	5 × 7 = 35	28 ÷ 7 = 4
4 × 7 = 28	9 × 7 = 63	56 ÷ 7 = 8
5 × 7 = 35	4 × 7 = 28	42 ÷ 7 = 6
6 × 7 = 42	10 × 7 = 70	63 ÷ 7 = 9
7 × 7 = 49	3 × 7 = 21	21 ÷ 7 = 3
8 × 7 = 56	1 × 7 = 7	49 ÷ 7 = 7
9 × 7 = 63	7 × 7 = 49	7 ÷ 7 = 1
10 × 7 = 70	2 × 7 = 14	35 ÷ 7 = 5

8s

Count-bys	Mixed Up ×	Mixed Up ÷
1 × 8 = 8	6 × 8 = 48	16 ÷ 8 = 2
2 × 8 = 16	10 × 8 = 80	40 ÷ 8 = 5
3 × 8 = 24	7 × 8 = 56	72 ÷ 8 = 9
4 × 8 = 32	2 × 8 = 16	32 ÷ 8 = 4
5 × 8 = 40	4 × 8 = 32	8 ÷ 8 = 1
6 × 8 = 48	8 × 8 = 64	80 ÷ 8 = 10
7 × 8 = 56	5 × 8 = 40	64 ÷ 8 = 8
8 × 8 = 64	10 × 8 = 80	24 ÷ 8 = 3
9 × 8 = 72	3 × 8 = 24	56 ÷ 8 = 7
10 × 8 = 80	1 × 8 = 8	48 ÷ 8 = 6

squares

Count-bys	Mixed Up ×	Mixed Up ÷
1 × 1 = 1	3 × 3 = 9	25 ÷ 5 = 5
2 × 2 = 4	9 × 9 = 81	4 ÷ = 2
3 × 3 = 9	4 × 4 = 16	= 9
4 × 4 = 16	6 × 6 = 36	÷ 3 = 3
5 × 5 = 25	2 × 2 =	36 ÷ 6 = 6
6 × 6 = 36	= 100	100 ÷ 10 = 10
7 × 7 = 49		16 ÷ 4 = 4
8 × 8 =	1 × 1 = 1	49 ÷ 7 = 7
9 ×	× 5 = 25	1 ÷ 1 = 1
	8 × 8 = 64	64 ÷ 8 = 8

Homework

Name

Date

Multiply or divide to find the unknown numbers.
Then check your answers at the bottom of this page.

1. $6 \times 6 = \boxed{}$

2. $20 \div 4 = \boxed{}$

3. $9 * 9 = \boxed{}$

4. $32 / 4 = \boxed{}$

5. $9 \bullet \boxed{} = 54$

6. $\frac{30}{10} = \boxed{}$

7. $5 \times 0 = \boxed{}$

8. $\frac{48}{6} = \boxed{}$

9. $3 \times 6 = \boxed{}$

10. $6\overline{)30}$

11. $8 \bullet 4 = \boxed{}$

12. $12 \div 6 = \boxed{}$

13. $6 * \boxed{} = 42$

14. $\frac{6}{6} = \boxed{}$

15. $3 \bullet 4 = \boxed{}$

16. $15 / 5 = \boxed{}$

17. $10 \div 10 = \boxed{}$

18. $2 * 7 = \boxed{}$

19. $\boxed{} \times 2 = 10$

20. $6\overline{)18}$

21. $10 \times \boxed{} = 70$

1. 36 2. 5 3. 81 4. 8 5. 6 6. 3 7. 0 8. 8 9. 18 10. 5 11. 32 12. 2 13. 7 14. 1 15. 12 16. 3 17. 1 18. 14 19. 5 20. 3 21. 7

Solve Area Word Problems

Homework

Use this chart to practice your 8s count-bys, multiplications, and divisions. Then have your Homework Helper test you.

8s	× In Order	× Mixed Up	÷ Mixed Up
	$1 \times 8 = 8$	$3 \times 8 = 24$	$40 \div 8 = 5$
	$2 \times 8 = 16$	$9 \times 8 = 72$	$56 \div 8 = 7$
	$3 \times 8 = 24$	$6 \times 8 = 48$	$24 \div 8 = 3$
	$4 \times 8 = 32$	$4 \times 8 = 32$	$72 \div 8 = 9$
	$5 \times 8 = 40$	$2 \times 8 = 16$	$8 \div 8 = 1$
	$6 \times 8 = 48$	$8 \times 8 = 64$	$48 \div 8 = 6$
	$7 \times 8 = 56$	$1 \times 8 = 8$	$32 \div 8 = 4$
	$8 \times 8 = 64$	$5 \times 8 = 40$	$64 \div 8 = 8$
	$9 \times 8 = 72$	$10 \times 8 = 80$	$16 \div 8 = 2$
	$10 \times 8 = 80$	$7 \times 8 = 56$	$80 \div 8 = 10$

Home Check Sheet 7: 6s and 8s

6s Multiplications	6s Divisions	8s Multiplications	8s Divisions
$10 \times 6 = 60$	$24 / 6 = 4$	$2 \times 8 = 16$	$72 / 8 = 9$
$6 \cdot 4 = 24$	$48 \div 6 = 8$	$8 \cdot 10 = 80$	$16 \div 8 = 2$
$6 * 7 = 42$	$60 / 6 = 10$	$3 * 8 = 24$	$40 / 8 = 5$
$2 \times 6 = 12$	$12 \div 6 = 2$	$9 \times 8 = 72$	$8 \div 8 = 1$
$6 \cdot 5 = 30$	$42 / 6 = 7$	$8 \cdot 4 = 32$	$80 / 8 = 10$
$6 * 8 = 48$	$30 \div 6 = 5$	$8 * 7 = 56$	$48 \div 8 = 6$
$9 \times 6 = 54$	$6 / 6 = 1$	$5 \times 8 = 40$	$56 / 8 = 7$
$6 \cdot 1 = 6$	$18 \div 6 = 3$	$8 \cdot 6 = 48$	$24 \div 8 = 3$
$6 * 6 = 36$	$54 / 6 = 9$	$1 * 8 = 8$	$64 / 8 = 8$
$6 \times 3 = 18$	$36 / 6 = 6$	$8 \times 8 = 64$	$32 / 8 = 4$
$6 \cdot 6 = 36$	$48 \div 6 = 8$	$4 \cdot 8 = 32$	$80 \div 8 = 10$
$5 * 6 = 30$	$12 / 6 = 2$	$6 * 8 = 48$	$56 / 8 = 7$
$6 \times 2 = 12$	$24 \div 6 = 4$	$8 \times 3 = 24$	$8 \div 8 = 1$
$4 \cdot 6 = 24$	$60 / 6 = 10$	$7 \cdot 8 = 56$	$24 / 8 = 3$
$6 * 9 = 54$	$6 \div 6 = 1$	$8 * 2 = 16$	$64 \div 8 = 8$
$8 \times 6 = 48$	$42 / 6 = 7$	$8 \times 9 = 72$	$16 / 8 = 2$
$7 \cdot 6 = 42$	$18 \div 6 = 3$	$8 \cdot 1 = 8$	$72 \div 8 = 9$
$6 * 10 = 60$	$36 \div 6 = 6$	$8 * 8 = 64$	$32 \div 8 = 4$
$1 \times 6 = 6$	$30 / 6 = 5$	$10 \times 8 = 80$	$40 / 8 = 5$
$4 \cdot 6 = 24$	$54 \div 6 = 9$	$5 \cdot 8 = 40$	$48 \div 8 = 6$

Homework

Study Plan

Homework Helper

Find the unknown number for each Fast-Array Drawing.

1.

9
○○○○○○○○○
8 ○
 ○   ▢
 ○
 ○
 ○
 ○

2.

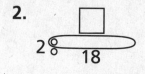

2 ○
 18

3.

7
○○○○○○
▢ ○
 35

Write an equation and solve the problem.

4. Tyrone planted 3 seeds every day for 8 days. How many seeds did Tyrone plant?

_____

5. There are 6 players on a volleyball team. How many players are in a game with 2 teams?

_____

6. Joseph gave his 6 nephews $48 for helping him clean out the garage. The boys divided the money equally. How much money did each boy get?

_____

7. Miki has 3 planting boxes for her flowers. Each box is 4 feet wide and 8 feet long. How much area for planting flowers does Miki have altogether?

_____

Name _____ Date _____

Remembering

Write an equation and solve the problem.   *Show your work.*

1. There are 0 tickets available. There are 6 people in line to purchase tickets. How many tickets did they purchase?

_____

Read each problem and decide what type of problem it is. Write the letter from the list below. Then write an equation and solve the problem.

   a. Array Multiplication
   b. Array Division
   c. Equal Groups of Multiplication
   d. Equal Groups Division with Unknown Group Size
   e. Equal Groups Division with an Unknown Multiplier (number of groups)

2. Owen orders 9 boxes of hammers for the hardware store. Each box has 10 hammers. How many hammers does Owen order?

_____

3. Tameka has 12 granola bars for the bake sale. She puts 4 granola bars on each plate. How many plates does she fill?

_____

Complete each Unknown Number puzzle.

4.

×		5	
	12		36
6			
2	6		

5.

×	2		6
		45	
3		27	
		63	42

6.

×		7	3
		20	15
9		63	
		24	

7. **Stretch Your Thinking** A pizza parlor has 8 different toppings and 3 different cheeses to choose from on the menu. How many pizza combinations are possible if each pizza has 1 topping and 1 cheese?

_____

Multiply and Divide with 8

Study Plan

_____

Homework Helper

Solve. Then circle what type it is and what operation you used.

1. The area of a photograph is 15 square inches. If the width of the photograph is 3 inches, what is its length?

_____

array   equal groups   area

multiplication   division

2. Mrs. Divita divided 64 beetles equally among the 8 students in the science club. How many beetles did each student receive?

_____

array   equal groups   area

multiplication   division

3. Write your own problem that is the same type as Problem 1.

_____
_____
_____

4. Write your own problem that is the same type as Problem 2.

_____
_____
_____

Find the unknown number for each Fast-Array Drawing.

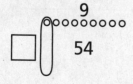

5.   9
☐ 54

6.   4
7 ☐

7.   ☐
6 36

Name _____   **Date** _____

Remembering

Write an equation and solve the problem.   *Show your work.*

1. Lucy puts 54 pictures in her photo album. She puts 9 photos on each page. How many pages does she fill?

   _____

2. Chris sets up 8 chairs in each row. He sets up 7 rows. How many chairs does Chris set up?

   _____

3. Trina places 4 peaches in each gift basket. She puts together 9 gift baskets to sell in her store. How many peaches does Trina use?

   _____

4. Jorge has 15 science fair awards. He wants to display the same number of awards among 3 shelves. How many awards should he put on each shelf?

   _____

Find the unknown number for each Fast Array Drawing.

5.

6.

7.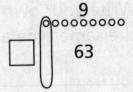

8. **Stretch Your Thinking** Write a real world problem and equation using $t = 5$.

   _____

   _____

   _____

Write Word Problems and Equations

Homework

Use this chart to practice your 7s count-bys, multiplications, and divisions. Then have your Homework Helper test you.

	× In Order	× Mixed Up	÷ Mixed Up
7s	$1 \times 7 = 7$	$5 \times 7 = 35$	$56 \div 7 = 8$
	$2 \times 7 = 14$	$1 \times 7 = 7$	$42 \div 7 = 6$
	$3 \times 7 = 21$	$10 \times 7 = 70$	$14 \div 7 = 2$
	$4 \times 7 = 28$	$2 \times 7 = 14$	$7 \div 7 = 1$
	$5 \times 7 = 35$	$9 \times 7 = 63$	$70 \div 7 = 10$
	$6 \times 7 = 42$	$3 \times 7 = 21$	$49 \div 7 = 7$
	$7 \times 7 = 49$	$8 \times 7 = 56$	$21 \div 7 = 3$
	$8 \times 7 = 56$	$4 \times 7 = 28$	$35 \div 7 = 5$
	$9 \times 7 = 63$	$7 \times 7 = 49$	$63 \div 7 = 9$
	$10 \times 7 = 70$	$6 \times 7 = 42$	$28 \div 7 = 4$

Homework

Multiply or divide to find the unknown numbers. Then check your answers at the bottom of this page.

1. $7 \times 7 = \boxed{}$

2. $\dfrac{64}{8} = \boxed{}$

3. $5 \times 5 = \boxed{}$

4. $28 / 7 = \boxed{}$

5. $9 \cdot \boxed{} = 27$

6. $\dfrac{48}{6} = \boxed{}$

7. $\boxed{} \times 9 = 63$

8. $7\overline{)56}$ $\boxed{}$

9. $10 \times \boxed{} = 30$

10. $8 \times 5 = \boxed{}$

11. $21 \div 3 = \boxed{}$

12. $9 * 2 = \boxed{}$

13. $30 / 6 = \boxed{}$

14. $8 \cdot 5 = \boxed{}$

15. $24 \div 3 = \boxed{}$

16. $3\overline{)21}$ $\boxed{}$

17. $90 \div 9 = \boxed{}$

18. $2 * 7 = \boxed{}$

19. $6 * \boxed{} = 42$

20. $\dfrac{10}{2} = \boxed{}$

21. $3 \cdot 9 = \boxed{}$

1. 49 2. 8 3. 25 4. 4 5. 3 6. 8 7. 7 8. 8 9. 3 10. 40 11. 7
12. 18 13. 5 14. 40 15. 8 16. 7 17. 10 18. 14 19. 7 20. 5 21. 27

Multiply and Divide with 7

Homework

Study Plan

_____

Homework Helper

Find the unknown number for each Fast-Array Drawing.

1. □ 7 ∘∘∘∘∘∘∘
    21

2. 9 ∘∘∘∘∘∘∘∘∘
    5 ∘ □
      ∘
      ∘
      ∘

3. □
    5 ∘ 35

4. 9 ∘∘∘∘∘∘∘∘∘
    8 ∘ □
      ∘
      ∘
      ∘

5. 9 ∘∘∘∘∘∘∘∘
    □ 45

6. □
    7 ∘ 49
      ∘
      ∘
      ∘

Solve. Label your answers.

7. Rachel plans to fence in an area 7 meters long by 7 meters wide for her dog to run in. How much area will her dog have to run in?

8. Shondra has 21 tropical fish. If she divides them evenly among 3 tanks, how many fish will be in each tank?

9. Write a word problem that involves an array and multiplication. Write your problem on a separate sheet of paper for your teacher to collect.

Remembering

Write an equation and solve the problem.

Show your work.

1. Sara picks 48 apples. She puts 6 apples in each basket. How many baskets does she fill?

   _____

2. Mrs. Lin places 5 pencils at each table in the classroom. There are 7 tables in the classroom. How many pencils does Mrs. Lin place on the tables?

   _____

3. Gibson has an assignment to read 8 pages in his reading book. It takes him 2 minutes to read each page. How many minutes will it take him to finish the reading assignment?

   _____

4. There are 4 paper towel rolls in each package. There are 7 packages of paper towel rolls on the shelf. How many paper towel rolls are on the shelf?

   _____

Solve. Then circle what type it is and what operation you used.

5. The area of the paper is 80 square inches. If the width of the paper is 8 inches, what is its length?

   _____

   array   equal groups   area

   multiplication   division

6. The desks are in 6 rows, with 5 desks in each row. How many desks are in the classroom?

   _____

   array   equal groups   area

   multiplication   division

7. **Stretch Your Thinking** Write a word problem using 7 groups. Solve your problem.

   _____

   _____

Multiply and Divide with 7

Homework

Home Check Sheet 8: 7s and Squares

7s Multiplications	7s Divisions	Squares Multiplications	Squares Divisions
$4 \times 7 = 28$	$14 / 7 = 2$	$8 \times 8 = 64$	$81 / 9 = 9$
$7 \cdot 2 = 14$	$28 \div 7 = 4$	$10 \cdot 10 = 100$	$4 \div 2 = 2$
$7 * 8 = 56$	$70 / 7 = 10$	$3 * 3 = 9$	$25 / 5 = 5$
$7 \times 7 = 49$	$56 \div 7 = 8$	$9 \times 9 = 81$	$1 \div 1 = 1$
$7 \cdot 1 = 7$	$42 / 7 = 6$	$4 \cdot 4 = 16$	$100 / 10 = 10$
$7 * 10 = 70$	$63 \div 7 = 9$	$7 * 7 = 49$	$36 \div 6 = 6$
$3 \times 7 = 21$	$7 / 7 = 1$	$5 \times 5 = 25$	$49 / 7 = 7$
$7 \cdot 6 = 42$	$49 \div 7 = 7$	$6 \cdot 6 = 36$	$9 \div 3 = 3$
$5 * 7 = 35$	$21 / 7 = 3$	$1 * 1 = 1$	$64 / 8 = 8$
$7 \times 9 = 63$	$35 / 7 = 5$	$5 * 5 = 25$	$16 / 4 = 4$
$7 \cdot 4 = 28$	$7 \div 7 = 1$	$1 \cdot 1 = 1$	$100 \div 10 = 10$
$9 * 7 = 63$	$63 / 7 = 9$	$3 \cdot 3 = 9$	$49 / 7 = 7$
$2 \times 7 = 14$	$14 \div 7 = 2$	$10 \times 10 = 100$	$1 \div 1 = 1$
$7 \cdot 5 = 35$	$70 / 7 = 10$	$4 \times 4 = 16$	$9 / 3 = 3$
$8 * 7 = 56$	$21 \div 7 = 3$	$9 * 9 = 81$	$64 \div 8 = 8$
$7 \times 3 = 21$	$49 / 7 = 7$	$2 \times 2 = 4$	$4 / 2 = 2$
$6 \cdot 7 = 42$	$28 \div 7 = 4$	$6 * 6 = 36$	$81 \div 9 = 9$
$10 * 7 = 70$	$56 \div 7 = 8$	$7 \times 7 = 49$	$16 \div 4 = 4$
$1 \times 7 = 7$	$35 / 7 = 5$	$5 \cdot 5 = 25$	$25 / 5 = 5$
$7 \cdot 7 = 49$	$42 \div 7 = 6$	$8 \cdot 8 = 64$	$36 \div 6 = 6$

Homework

Multiply or divide to find the unknown numbers. Then check your answers at the bottom of this page.

1. $\boxed{} \times 6 = 48$

2. $56 \div 7 = \boxed{}$

3. $10 \times \boxed{} = 90$

4. $64 / 8 = \boxed{}$

5. $9 \bullet \boxed{} = 63$

6. $\frac{25}{5} = \boxed{}$

7. $8 \times 9 = \boxed{}$

8. $9)\overline{36}$ with $\boxed{}$ above

9. $7 * 7 = \boxed{}$

10. $6 * \boxed{} = 36$

11. $\frac{32}{4} = \boxed{}$

12. $3 \bullet 3 = \boxed{}$

13. $30 / 6 = \boxed{}$

14. $16 \div 4 = \boxed{}$

15. $8 * 5 = \boxed{}$

16. $6 \times 4 = \boxed{}$

17. $\frac{81}{9} = \boxed{}$

18. $5 \times 7 = \boxed{}$

19. $60 / 6 = \boxed{}$

20. $7 \bullet 8 = \boxed{}$

21. $42 \div 7 = \boxed{}$

22. $6)\overline{54}$ with $\boxed{}$ above

23. $32 \div 8 = \boxed{}$

24. $9 * 9 = \boxed{}$

23. 4 24. 81
13. 5 14. 4 15. 40 16. 24 17. 9 18. 35 19. 10 20. 56 21. 6 22. 9
1. 8 2. 8 3. 9 4. 8 5. 7 6. 5 7. 72 8. 4 9. 49 10. 6 11. 8 12. 9

© Houghton Mifflin Harcourt Publishing Company

Square Numbers

Homework

Name _____   Date _____

Home Check Sheet 9: 6s, 7s, and 8s

6s, 7s, and 8s Multiplications	6s, 7s, and 8s Multiplications	6s, 7s, and 8s Divisions	6s, 7s, and 8s Divisions
$1 \times 6 = 6$	$0 \times 8 = 0$	$24 / 6 = 4$	$54 / 6 = 9$
$6 \cdot 7 = 42$	$6 \cdot 2 = 12$	$21 \div 7 = 3$	$24 \div 8 = 3$
$3 * 8 = 24$	$4 * 7 = 28$	$16 / 8 = 2$	$14 / 7 = 2$
$6 \times 2 = 12$	$8 \times 3 = 24$	$24 \div 8 = 3$	$32 \div 8 = 4$
$7 \cdot 5 = 35$	$5 \cdot 6 = 30$	$14 / 7 = 2$	$18 / 6 = 3$
$8 * 4 = 32$	$7 * 2 = 14$	$30 \div 6 = 5$	$56 \div 7 = 8$
$6 \times 6 = 36$	$3 \times 8 = 24$	$35 / 7 = 5$	$40 / 8 = 5$
$8 \cdot 7 = 56$	$6 \cdot 4 = 24$	$24 \div 8 = 3$	$35 \div 7 = 5$
$9 * 8 = 72$	$0 * 7 = 0$	$18 / 6 = 3$	$12 / 6 = 2$
$6 \times 10 = 60$	$8 \times 1 = 8$	$12 / 6 = 2$	$21 / 7 = 3$
$7 \cdot 1 = 7$	$8 \cdot 6 = 48$	$42 \div 7 = 6$	$16 \div 8 = 2$
$8 * 3 = 24$	$7 * 9 = 63$	$56 / 8 = 7$	$42 / 6 = 7$
$5 \times 6 = 30$	$10 \times 8 = 80$	$49 \div 7 = 7$	$80 \div 8 = 10$
$4 \cdot 7 = 28$	$6 \cdot 10 = 60$	$16 / 8 = 2$	$36 / 6 = 6$
$2 * 8 = 16$	$3 * 7 = 21$	$60 \div 6 = 10$	$7 \div 7 = 1$
$7 \times 7 = 49$	$8 \times 4 = 32$	$54 / 6 = 9$	$64 / 8 = 8$
$7 \cdot 6 = 42$	$6 \cdot 5 = 30$	$8 \div 8 = 1$	$24 \div 6 = 4$
$8 * 8 = 64$	$7 * 4 = 28$	$28 \div 7 = 4$	$21 \div 7 = 3$
$9 \times 6 = 54$	$8 \times 8 = 64$	$72 / 8 = 9$	$49 / 7 = 7$
$10 \cdot 7 = 70$	$6 \cdot 9 = 54$	$56 \div 7 = 8$	$24 \div 8 = 3$

Homework

Name _____   Date _____

Home Check Sheet 10: 0s–10s

0s–10s Multiplications	0s–10s Multiplications	0s–10s Divisions	0s–10s Divisions
0 × 0 = 0	9 × 4 = 36	9 / 1 = 9	90 / 10 = 9
1 • 1 = 1	5 • 9 = 45	12 ÷ 3 = 4	64 ÷ 8 = 8
2 * 3 = 6	6 * 10 = 60	14 / 2 = 7	15 / 5 = 3
1 × 3 = 3	7 × 3 = 21	20 ÷ 4 = 5	12 ÷ 6 = 2
5 • 4 = 20	5 • 3 = 15	10 / 5 = 2	14 / 7 = 2
7 * 5 = 35	4 * 1 = 4	48 ÷ 8 = 6	45 ÷ 9 = 5
6 × 9 = 54	7 × 5 = 35	35 / 7 = 5	8 / 1 = 8
4 • 7 = 28	6 • 3 = 18	60 ÷ 6 = 10	30 ÷ 3 = 10
1 * 8 = 8	8 * 7 = 56	81 / 9 = 9	16 / 4 = 4
9 × 8 = 72	5 × 8 = 40	20 / 10 = 2	8 / 2 = 4
2 • 10 = 20	9 • 9 = 81	16 ÷ 2 = 8	80 ÷ 10 = 8
0 * 7 = 0	9 * 10 = 90	30 / 5 = 6	36 / 4 = 9
4 × 1 = 4	0 × 0 = 0	49 ÷ 7 = 7	25 ÷ 5 = 5
2 • 4 = 8	1 • 0 = 0	60 / 6 = 10	42 / 7 = 6
10 * 3 = 30	1 * 6 = 6	30 ÷ 3 = 10	36 ÷ 6 = 6
8 × 4 = 32	7 × 2 = 14	8 / 1 = 8	90 / 9 = 10
5 • 8 = 40	6 • 3 = 18	16 ÷ 4 = 4	24 ÷ 8 = 3
4 * 6 = 24	4 * 5 = 20	16 ÷ 8 = 2	6 ÷ 2 = 3
7 × 6 = 42	6 × 6 = 36	40 / 10 = 4	9 / 3 = 3
1 • 8 = 8	10 • 7 = 70	36 ÷ 9 = 4	1 ÷ 1 = 1

Homework

Name	Date

Study Plan

Homework Helper

Solve.

1. Sarah's chickens laid 3 dozen eggs over the weekend. She divided them equally into cartons to give away to her 6 closest neighbors. How many eggs did she put in each carton?

_____

2. Latisha needs 60 square feet of cloth. She has a rectangular piece of cloth that measures 3 feet by 9 feet, and a square piece that measures 5 feet on a side. Does she have enough cloth? If not, how much more does she need?

_____

3. Lucy has 6 sheets of stickers. Each sheet has 8 stickers. How many stickers does Lucy have?

_____

4. A park ranger led 3 groups of hikers. There were 7 people in each group. How many hikers did she lead?

_____

Find the unknown number for each Fast-Array.

5.

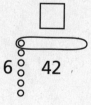

6   42

6.

6

54

7.

8

7

Name _____ **Date** _____

Remembering

Write an equation and solve the problem.

1. Adam has 60 plates. He places 10 plates on each table. How many tables does Adam place plates on?

   _____

2. Hailey draws 35 leaves on her tree. She draws 5 leaves on each branch. How many branches are on her tree?

   _____

Find the unknown number for each Fast Array Drawing.

3.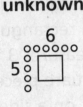

4.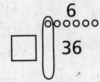

5.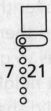

Write a multiplication equation for each array.

  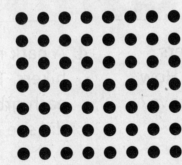 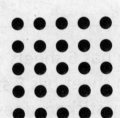

6. _____   7. _____   8. _____

9. **Stretch Your Thinking** Draw a picture to show 7×7.

Practice with 6s, 7s, and 8s

Homework

> **Study Plan**
>
>
> Homework Helper

Write an equation to solve the problem.

1. Maria created artwork by placing all of her seashells in 4 rows on a wall. In each row, she arranged 8 seashells. How many seashells did Maria collect in all?

   _____

2. Arturo collected 18 seashells. He wants to divide the seashells evenly among his 3 best friends. How many seashells will each friend receive?

   _____

Use the pictograph and key to solve.

Katie planted pumpkins in the spring. Now she is selling them. This pictograph shows how many pumpkins she sold this weekend.

Friday	🎃 🎃 🎃 🎃
Saturday	🎃 🎃 🎃 🎃 🎃 🎃 🎃
Sunday	🎃 🎃 🎃

Key: 🎃 = 6 pumpkins

3. How many pumpkins did Katie sell on Friday?

   _____

4. How many more pumpkins did she sell on Saturday than on Friday?

   _____

5. How many pumpkins did Katie sell this weekend?

   _____

Remembering

Write an equation and solve the problem.

1. The fitness instructor puts the class into 10 rows. There are 6 people in each row. How many people are in the class?

_____

2. Jared has 40 stars. He puts the same number of stars in each of 5 rows. How many stars are in each row?

Write a multiplication equation for each array.

  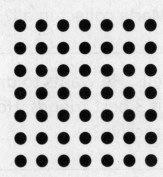 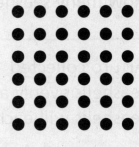

3. _____ **4.** _____ **5.** _____

Solve.

6. Amanda has 8 boxes of markers. Each box has 7 markers. How many markers in all are in the boxes?

_____

7. Alex has 7 shirts. He sews 6 buttons on each shirt. How many buttons does Alex sew on the shirts?

_____

8. Stretch Your Thinking Write a word problem with 16 for the product.

_____

_____

_____

Building Fluency with 0s–10s

Homework

Study Plan

_____

Homework Helper

Write an equation and solve the problem.

1. Shamariah collects silk roses. She had 17 silk roses in a vase. Six friends each gave her 3 more roses. How many roses does Shamariah have now?

_____

2. Takala put 9 marbles in the box, Jackie put in 7, and Laird put in 11. Then they divided the marbles evenly among themselves. How many did each person get?

_____

3. A pet store had 9 corn snakes. The snakes laid 8 eggs each. All but 5 of the eggs hatched. How many baby corn snakes does the pet store have?

_____

4. In a paper airplane contest, Amanda's plane flew 19 ft farther than Darren's plane. Darren's plane flew twice as far as Rachel's plane. Rachel's plane flew 20 ft. How far did Amanda's plane fly?

_____

5. Jenna divided 120 daisies into 2 equal groups. Then she divided each group equally into 10 small bunches. She gave her grandmother one small bunch. How many daisies did Jenna give her grandmother?

_____

Remembering

Write an equation and solve the problem.

1. Lily has 24 classmates. She gives each classmate 1 pencil. How many pencils in all does she give her classmates?

2. There are 50 students on a field trip. The tours let 10 students enter at a time. How many tours will be needed for each student to go on a tour?

_____

Write a question to finish the word problem. Then solve the problem.

3. The art teacher has 9 boxes of crayons. There are 8 crayons in each box.

Question: _____

_____

Solution: _____

Write the first step question and answer. Then solve the problem.

4. Mr. Garcia buys 8 packages of juice. There are 6 juice boxes in each package. On the field trip, 40 students drink a juice box. How many juice boxes are left?

_____

5. Stretch Your Thinking Write a two step word problem that uses multiplication and subtraction. Then solve the two step problem.

_____

_____

_____

_____

_____

Make Sense of Two Step Problems

2×2	$2 \cdot 3$	$2 * 4$	2×5
	Hint: What is $3 \cdot 2$?	Hint: What is $4 * 2$?	Hint: What is 5×2?

© Houghton Mifflin Harcourt Publishing Company

2×6	$2 \cdot 7$	$2 * 8$	2×9
Hint: What is 6×2?	Hint: What is $7 \cdot 2$?	Hint: What is $8 * 2$?	Hint: What is 9×2?

© Houghton Mifflin Harcourt Publishing Company

5×2	$5 \cdot 3$	$5 * 4$	5×5
Hint: What is 2×5?	Hint: What is $3 \cdot 5$?	Hint: What is $4 * 5$?	

© Houghton Mifflin Harcourt Publishing Company

5×6	$5 \cdot 7$	$5 * 8$	5×9
Hint: What is 6×5?	Hint: What is $7 \cdot 5$?	Hint: What is $8 * 5$?	Hint: What is 9×5?

© Houghton Mifflin Harcourt Publishing Company

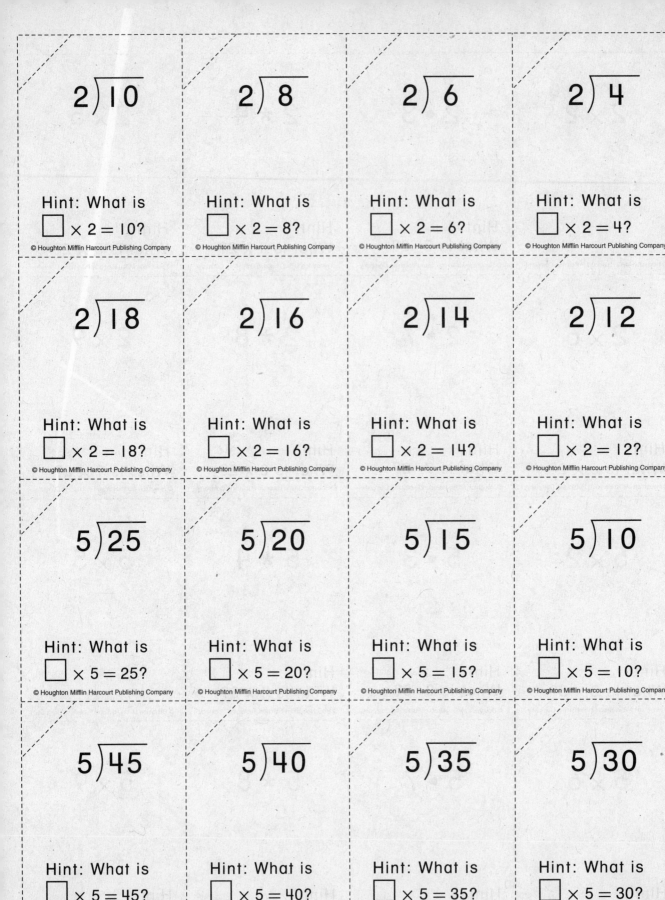

$2\overline{)10}$

Hint: What is
□ × 2 = 10?
© Houghton Mifflin Harcourt Publishing Company

$2\overline{)8}$

Hint: What is
□ × 2 = 8?
© Houghton Mifflin Harcourt Publishing Company

$2\overline{)6}$

Hint: What is
□ × 2 = 6?
© Houghton Mifflin Harcourt Publishing Company

$2\overline{)4}$

Hint: What is
□ × 2 = 4?
© Houghton Mifflin Harcourt Publishing Company

$2\overline{)18}$

Hint: What is
□ × 2 = 18?
© Houghton Mifflin Harcourt Publishing Company

$2\overline{)16}$

Hint: What is
□ × 2 = 16?
© Houghton Mifflin Harcourt Publishing Company

$2\overline{)14}$

Hint: What is
□ × 2 = 14?
© Houghton Mifflin Harcourt Publishing Company

$2\overline{)12}$

Hint: What is
□ × 2 = 12?
© Houghton Mifflin Harcourt Publishing Company

$5\overline{)25}$

Hint: What is
□ × 5 = 25?
© Houghton Mifflin Harcourt Publishing Company

$5\overline{)20}$

Hint: What is
□ × 5 = 20?
© Houghton Mifflin Harcourt Publishing Company

$5\overline{)15}$

Hint: What is
□ × 5 = 15?
© Houghton Mifflin Harcourt Publishing Company

$5\overline{)10}$

Hint: What is
□ × 5 = 10?
© Houghton Mifflin Harcourt Publishing Company

$5\overline{)45}$

Hint: What is
□ × 5 = 45?
© Houghton Mifflin Harcourt Publishing Company

$5\overline{)40}$

Hint: What is
□ × 5 = 40?
© Houghton Mifflin Harcourt Publishing Company

$5\overline{)35}$

Hint: What is
□ × 5 = 35?
© Houghton Mifflin Harcourt Publishing Company

$5\overline{)30}$

Hint: What is
□ × 5 = 30?
© Houghton Mifflin Harcourt Publishing Company

Home Product Cards: 2s, 5s, 9s

9 × 2

9 • 3

9 * 4

9 × 5

Hint:
What is 2 × 9?
© Houghton Mifflin Harcourt Publishing Company

Hint:
What is 3 • 9?
© Houghton Mifflin Harcourt Publishing Company

Hint:
What is 4 * 9?
© Houghton Mifflin Harcourt Publishing Company

Hint:
What is 5 × 9?
© Houghton Mifflin Harcourt Publishing Company

9 × 6

9 • 7

9 * 8

9 × 9

Hint:
What is 6 × 9?
© Houghton Mifflin Harcourt Publishing Company

Hint:
What is 7 • 9?
© Houghton Mifflin Harcourt Publishing Company

Hint:
What is 8 * 9?
© Houghton Mifflin Harcourt Publishing Company

© Houghton Mifflin Harcourt Publishing Company

×

•

*

×

×

•

*

×

You can write any numbers on the last 8 cards. Use them to practice difficult problems or if you lose a card.

Home Product Cards: 2s, 5s, 9s

$9\overline{)45}$ $9\overline{)36}$ $9\overline{)27}$ $9\overline{)18}$

Hint: What is
$\square \times 9 = 45$?
© Houghton Mifflin Harcourt Publishing Company

Hint: What is
$\square \times 9 = 36$?
© Houghton Mifflin Harcourt Publishing Company

Hint: What is
$\square \times 9 = 27$?
© Houghton Mifflin Harcourt Publishing Company

Hint: What is
$\square \times 9 = 18$?
© Houghton Mifflin Harcourt Publishing Company

$9\overline{)81}$ $9\overline{)72}$ $9\overline{)63}$ $9\overline{)54}$

Hint: What is
$\square \times 9 = 81$?
© Houghton Mifflin Harcourt Publishing Company

Hint: What is
$\square \times 9 = 72$?
© Houghton Mifflin Harcourt Publishing Company

Hint: What is
$\square \times 9 = 63$?
© Houghton Mifflin Harcourt Publishing Company

Hint: What is
$\square \times 9 = 54$?
© Houghton Mifflin Harcourt Publishing Company

You can write any numbers on the last 8 cards. Use them to practice difficult problems or if you lose a card.

Home Product Cards: 2s, 5s, 9s

3×2	$3 \cdot 3$	$3 * 4$	3×5
Hint: What is 2×3?	Hint: What is $3 \cdot 3$?	Hint: What is $4 * 3$?	Hint: What is 5×3?
© Houghton Mifflin Harcourt Publishing Company	© Houghton Mifflin Harcourt Publishing Company	© Houghton Mifflin Harcourt Publishing Company	© Houghton Mifflin Harcourt Publishing Company
3×6	$3 \cdot 7$	$3 * 8$	3×9
Hint: What is 6×3?	Hint: What is $7 \cdot 3$?	Hint: What is $8 * 3$?	Hint: What is 9×3?
© Houghton Mifflin Harcourt Publishing Company	© Houghton Mifflin Harcourt Publishing Company	© Houghton Mifflin Harcourt Publishing Company	© Houghton Mifflin Harcourt Publishing Company
4×2	$4 \cdot 3$	$4 * 4$	4×5
Hint: What is 2×4?	Hint: What is $3 \cdot 4$?	Hint: 	Hint: What is 5×4?
© Houghton Mifflin Harcourt Publishing Company	© Houghton Mifflin Harcourt Publishing Company	© Houghton Mifflin Harcourt Publishing Company	© Houghton Mifflin Harcourt Publishing Company
4×6	$4 \cdot 7$	$4 * 8$	4×9
Hint: What is 6×4?	Hint: What is $7 \cdot 4$?	Hint: What is $8 * 4$?	Hint: What is 9×4?
© Houghton Mifflin Harcourt Publishing Company	© Houghton Mifflin Harcourt Publishing Company	© Houghton Mifflin Harcourt Publishing Company	© Houghton Mifflin Harcourt Publishing Company

© Houghton Mifflin Harcourt Publishing Company

UNIT 2 LESSON 13

Home Product Cards: 3s, 4s **137**

$3\overline{)15}$ $3\overline{)12}$ $3\overline{)9}$ $3\overline{)6}$

Hint: What is
$\square \times 3 = 15?$
© Houghton Mifflin Harcourt Publishing Company

Hint: What is
$\square \times 3 = 12?$
© Houghton Mifflin Harcourt Publishing Company

Hint: What is
$\square \times 3 = 9?$
© Houghton Mifflin Harcourt Publishing Company

Hint: What is
$\square \times 3 = 6?$
© Houghton Mifflin Harcourt Publishing Company

$3\overline{)27}$ $3\overline{)24}$ $3\overline{)21}$ $3\overline{)18}$

Hint: What is
$\square \times 3 = 27?$
© Houghton Mifflin Harcourt Publishing Company

Hint: What is
$\square \times 3 = 24?$
© Houghton Mifflin Harcourt Publishing Company

Hint: What is
$\square \times 3 = 21?$
© Houghton Mifflin Harcourt Publishing Company

Hint: What is
$\square \times 3 = 18?$
© Houghton Mifflin Harcourt Publishing Company

$4\overline{)20}$ $4\overline{)16}$ $4\overline{)12}$ $4\overline{)8}$

Hint: What is
$\square \times 4 = 20?$
© Houghton Mifflin Harcourt Publishing Company

Hint: What is
$\square \times 4 = 16?$
© Houghton Mifflin Harcourt Publishing Company

Hint: What is
$\square \times 4 = 12?$
© Houghton Mifflin Harcourt Publishing Company

Hint: What is
$\square \times 4 = 8?$
© Houghton Mifflin Harcourt Publishing Company

$4\overline{)36}$ $4\overline{)32}$ $4\overline{)28}$ $4\overline{)24}$

Hint: What is
$\square \times 4 = 36?$
© Houghton Mifflin Harcourt Publishing Company

Hint: What is
$\square \times 4 = 32?$
© Houghton Mifflin Harcourt Publishing Company

Hint: What is
$\square \times 4 = 28?$
© Houghton Mifflin Harcourt Publishing Company

Hint: What is
$\square \times 4 = 24?$
© Houghton Mifflin Harcourt Publishing Company

© Houghton Mifflin Harcourt Publishing Company

Home Product Cards: 3s, 4s

8×2	$8 \cdot 3$	$8 * 4$	8×5

Hint:
What is 2×8?

Hint:
What is $3 \cdot 8$?

Hint:
What is $4 * 8$?

Hint:
What is 5×8?

8×6	$8 \cdot 7$	$8 * 8$	8×9

Hint:
What is 6×8?

Hint:
What is $7 \cdot 8$?

Hint:

Hint:
What is 9×8?

$\times$	$\bullet$	$*$	$\times$

$\times$	$\bullet$	$*$	$\times$

You can write any numbers on the last 8 cards. Use them to practice difficult problems or if you lose a card.

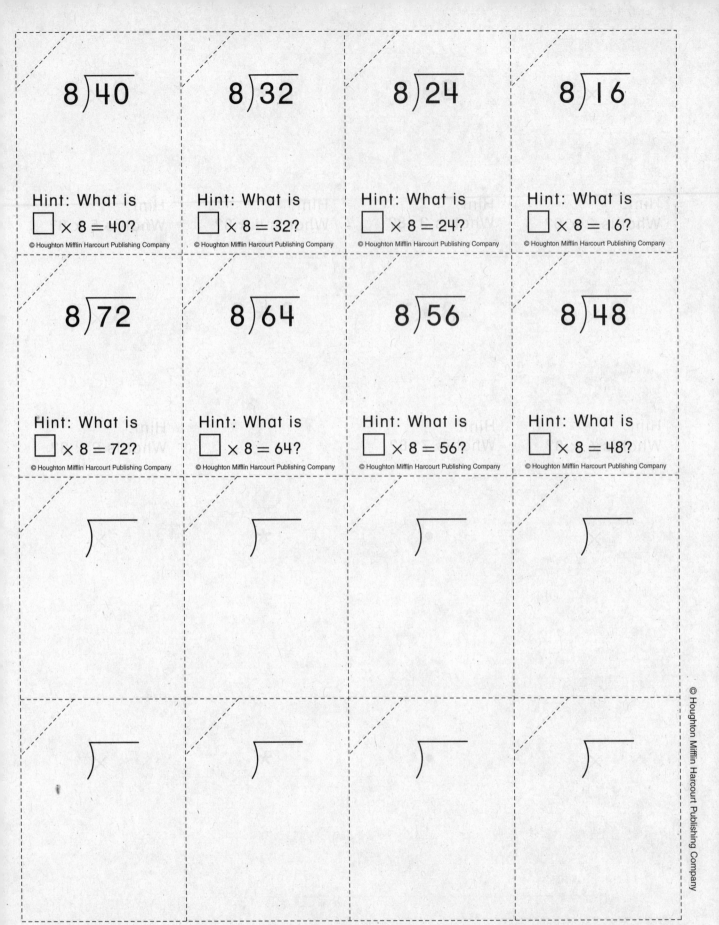

$8\overline{)40}$

Hint: What is

☐ $\times\, 8 = 40$?

© Houghton Mifflin Harcourt Publishing Company

$8\overline{)32}$

Hint: What is

☐ $\times\, 8 = 32$?

© Houghton Mifflin Harcourt Publishing Company

$8\overline{)24}$

Hint: What is

☐ $\times\, 8 = 24$?

© Houghton Mifflin Harcourt Publishing Company

$8\overline{)16}$

Hint: What is

☐ $\times\, 8 = 16$?

© Houghton Mifflin Harcourt Publishing Company

$8\overline{)72}$

Hint: What is

☐ $\times\, 8 = 72$?

© Houghton Mifflin Harcourt Publishing Company

$8\overline{)64}$

Hint: What is

☐ $\times\, 8 = 64$?

© Houghton Mifflin Harcourt Publishing Company

$8\overline{)56}$

Hint: What is

☐ $\times\, 8 = 56$?

© Houghton Mifflin Harcourt Publishing Company

$8\overline{)48}$

Hint: What is

☐ $\times\, 8 = 48$?

© Houghton Mifflin Harcourt Publishing Company

You can write any numbers on the last 8 cards. Use them to practice difficult problems or if you lose a card.

Home Product Cards: 6s, 7s, 8s

Homework

Study Plan

Homework Helper

Complete.

1. $6 \times 3 =$ _____

2. $7 \times 9 =$ _____

3. $4 \times 0 =$ _____

4. $30 \div 5 =$ _____

5. $18 \div 2 =$ _____

6. $70 \div 7 =$ _____

7. $36 \div$ _____ $= 9$

8. $3 \times$ _____ $= 24$

9. _____ $\div 8 = 0$

10. _____ $\times 7 = 35$

11. $60 =$ _____ $\times 6$

12. $4 = 28 \div$ _____

13. $72 = 8 \times$ _____

14. $2 =$ _____ $\div 10$

15. _____ $= 45 \div 9$

16. $21 =$ _____ $\times 7$

17. $8 = 64 \div$ _____

18. _____ $\times 374 = 0$

Solve.

19. Using only whole numbers, Nikki wrote as
many multiplication equations as she could
with 12 as the product. What were her equations?

_____

_____

20. Pablo wrote four division equations with 6
as the quotient. What could have been the four
division equations that he wrote?

_____

_____

Remembering

Write an equation and solve the problem.

1. Stephen has a stamp collection of 72 stamps. He puts 9 stamps on each page in his album. How many pages does he fill?

_____

2. There are 6 birdcages at the zoo. Two birds are in each birdcage. How many birds are in the birdcages?

_____

Use a basic multiplication and mental math to complete.

3. $2 \times 8 =$ _____

   $20 \times 8 =$ _____

4. $5 \times 9 =$ _____

   $5 \times 90 =$ _____

5. $3 \times 7 =$ _____

   $30 \times 7 =$ _____

6. $6 \times 4 =$ _____

   $60 \times 4 =$ _____

7. $9 \times 4 =$ _____

   $9 \times 40 =$ _____

8. $5 \times 5 =$ _____

   $50 \times 5 =$ _____

9. $7 \times 80 =$ _____

10. $70 \times 7 =$ _____

11. $6 \times 60 =$ _____

Write an equation and solve the problem.

12. Max has $12 for the field trip. Sue has $4 less than Max. Ellen has $2 more than Sue. How much money does Ellen have for the field trip?

_____

13. Jeremiah mows 8 lawns. Andy mows 4 fewer lawns than Jeremiah. Sally mows double the number Andy mows. How many lawns does Sally mow?

_____

14. **Stretch Your Thinking** Write three multiplication equations in which the product is 24. Then draw an array for one of your equations.

_____

Homework

A zoo kitchen's weekly grocery list shows the zoo orders 56 pounds of bananas each week. The zoo kitchen uses the same number of pounds of bananas each day.

1. Complete the chart showing the number of pounds of bananas the zoo kitchen has used after each day of the week.

Number of Days	1	2	3	4	5	6	7
Number of Pounds of Bananas							56

2. Write an equation to show how to find the number of pounds of bananas the zoo uses in one day.

_____

Write an equation and solve the problem.

3. The zoo uses 10 pounds of apples each day. How many pounds of apples should be on the weekly grocery list?

_____

4. After 6 days, how many pounds of apples does the zoo use?

_____

5. After 6 days, how many more pounds of apples than bananas does the zoo use?

_____

6. How many pounds of bananas and apples altogether does the zoo use each week?

_____

Remembering

Write an equation and solve the problem.

1. Tami uses square tiles to make an array. She places 5 tiles in each row. She makes 5 rows. How many square tiles does she use?

_____

2. Mrs. Gibbs sets up 36 chairs for parents to watch the class performance. She makes 4 rows. How many chairs are in each row?

_____

Write an equation and solve the problem.

3. There are 163 adults and 37 students in the audience. Will 4 packages of 50 programs be enough for each person in the audience to receive a program? Explain.

_____

4. There were 8 rows of picture frames at the store. There are 7 picture frames in each row. Twelve picture frames are sold. How many picture frames are left at the store?

_____

Complete.

5. $40 \div 10 =$ _____

6. _____ $= 8 \times 3$

7. _____ $\times 4 = 28$

8. $2 \times 4 =$ _____

9. _____ $= 8 \times 8$

10. _____ $= 81 \div 9$

11. $9 \times 5 =$ _____

12. $42 \div$ _____ $= 6$

13. $9 \times$ _____ $= 63$

14. Stretch Your Thinking Matt runs four days a week. On the first day he runs 30 minutes. On the second day he runs 5 minutes more than on the first day. On the third day he runs the same number of minutes as the second day. On the fourth day he runs 10 minutes more than the previous day. After Matt runs on the fourth day, how many minutes in all has he run?

_____

Homework

**Estimate the length of the line segment in inches.
Then measure it to the nearest inch.**

1. ────────────────────────

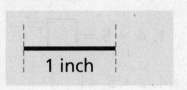

Estimate: _____ Actual: _____

**Estimate the length of the line segment in inches. Then
measure it to the nearest $\frac{1}{2}$ inch.**

2. ──────────────────

Estimate: _____ Actual: _____

**Estimate the length of each line segment in inches.
Then measure it to the nearest $\frac{1}{4}$ inch.**

3. ──────────

Estimate: _____ Actual: _____

4. ──────────────────────────────

Estimate: _____ Actual: _____

Draw a line segment that has the given length.

5. 4 inches

6. $3\frac{1}{4}$ inches

7. $4\frac{1}{2}$ inches

8. $\frac{3}{4}$ inch

9. Marta wants to make 4 necklaces that are the same
   length. She asks her friends to cut the string for the
   necklaces 15 paper clips long. Would all the lengths
   be the same? Explain your thinking.

   _____

   _____

Remembering

Solve each equation.

1. $4 \times 5 = \boxed{}$ 2. $10 * 5 = \boxed{}$ 3. $3 \cdot 5 = \boxed{}$

4. $2 * 5 = \boxed{}$ 5. $1 \cdot 5 = \boxed{}$ 6. $5 \times 9 = \boxed{}$

7. $5 \cdot 7 = \boxed{}$ 8. $5 * 5 = \boxed{}$ 9. $5 \times 6 = \boxed{}$

Solve each problem.

10. Tommy buys 6 notebooks. They cost $3 each. How much does he spend?

_____

11. Olivia has 42 muffins. She puts the same number of muffins into each of 6 baskets. How many muffins does Olivia put in each basket?

_____

Solve each problem. Label your answers with the correct units.

12. Ms. Emerson has a rectangular shelf that is 5 feet long and 3 feet wide. What is the area of the shelf?

_____

13. Trevor has a rectangular treasure box with an area of 72 square centimeters. If the length of one side is 9 centimeters, what is the length of the adjacent side?

_____

14. **Stretch Your Thinking** Grace has a piece of string that is 8 inches long. She needs to cut the string into four equal pieces, but she does not have a ruler. Explain a way Grace can cut the string into four equal pieces.

_____

_____

Customary Units of Length

1 liter (L) = 1,000 milliliters (mL)

Circle the better estimate.

1. a container of milk   2 L   20 mL

2. a cup of punch   25 L   250 mL

3. an eyedropper   1 L or 1 mL

4. a jar of pickles   50 L   500 mL

Choose the unit you would use to measure the liquid volume of each. Write *mL* or *L*.

5. a container of glue _____

6. an aquarium _____

Use the drawing to represent and solve the problem.

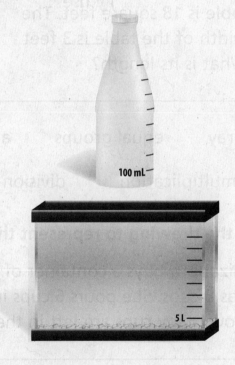

7. Dinah had a bottle of water that contained 800 milliliters of water. She used 500 milliliters. How much water is left in the bottle?

_____

8. Galen has a fish tank that holds 40 liters of water. He poured 15 liters of water into the tank. How many more liters does he need to add to fill the tank?

_____

Solve.

9. Ben has 4 hummingbird feeders. Each feeder holds 80 milliliters of liquid hummingbird food. How many milliliters of liquid hummingbird food does Ben need?

_____

10. Drew needs 27 liters of punch for a party. It comes in 3 liter containers. How many containers should Drew buy?

_____

Remembering

Make a math drawing for the problem and label it with a multiplication equation. Then write the answer to the problem.

1. Kelly's garden has 6 rows of tulips. There are 5 tulips in each row. How many tulips are in her garden?

   _____

Solve. Then circle what type it is and what operation you used.

2. The area of the rectangular table is 18 square feet. The width of the table is 3 feet. What is its length?

   _____

   array   equal groups   area

   multiplication   division

3. The band lines up in 8 rows, with 6 band members in each row. How many band members are there in all?

   _____

   array   equal groups   area

   multiplication   division

Use the drawing to represent the problem.

4. Elizabeth buys a container of orange juice that has 8 cups. She pours 6 cups into a pitcher. How many cups are left in the container?

   _____

1 cup

5. **Stretch Your Thinking** Write a word problem that involves subtracting 4 liters. Then solve. Draw a picture to represent your answer.

   _____

   _____

   _____

Homework

Solve. Use a clock or sketch a number line diagram if you need to.

1. Rhea arrived at the mall at 3:45 P.M. She spent 45 minutes having lunch and then she shopped for 55 minutes before leaving the mall. How much time did Rhea spend at the mall?

   _____

2. Mrs. Cox is baking a ham for dinner. It takes 1 hour 30 minutes to bake. The family eats at 6:15 P.M. What time should Mrs. Cox put the ham in the oven?

   _____

3. Dina started chores at 8:15 A.M. and finished at 9:05 A.M. It took her 30 minutes to clean her room and she spent the rest of the time bathing her dog. How long did Dina spend bathing her dog?

   _____

4. Jerry finished skating at 7:00 P.M. He skated for 1 hour 45 minutes. What time did he start skating?

   _____

5. Jason started his project at 2:30 P.M. and finished 2 hours and 15 minutes later. He spent 25 minutes doing research, 30 minutes writing a report, and the rest of the time building a model. What time did he finish his project? How much time did he spend building the model?

   _____

Remembering

Solve each problem.   *Show Your Work*

1. The farmer makes stacks of 4 bales of hay. He makes 6 stacks. How many bales of hay does he stack?

   _____

2. Lilly has 85 shells in her collection. She gives 13 shells to her best friend. She puts the rest of her shells in groups of 9. How many groups does she make?

   _____

Solve.

3. William and Hannah went to the bowling alley at 5:30 P.M. They bowled for 1 hour 20 minutes. Then they played a video game for 30 minutes. After the video game, they leave to go home. What time did they leave?

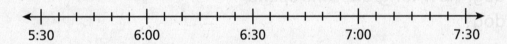

   5:30   6:00   6:30   7:00   7:30

   _____

4. **Stretch Your Thinking** Tony is cooking dinner. He starts cooking at different times, so all the foods will be ready at the same time. The chicken takes 25 minutes to cook, the rice takes 40 minutes to cook, and the green beans take 15 minutes to cook. All the foods are finished at 5:33 P.M. At what time did he start cooking each food?

   _____

   _____

Homework

Use the vertical bar graph to answer the questions.

Sunnytown Reading Festival

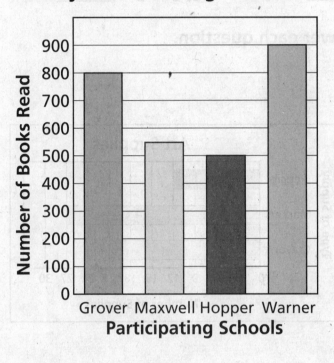

1. About how many books did students at Maxwell School read?

_____

2. How many more books did students at Grover School read than students at Hopper School?

_____

3. How many fewer books did students at Hopper School read than students at Warner School?

_____

4. How many more books did the students at Maxwell need to read to have the same number of books as Warner?

_____

5. Use the information in this table to make a vertical bar graph.

Pinball Scores

Player	Points
Trina	500
Mindy	350
Warren	200

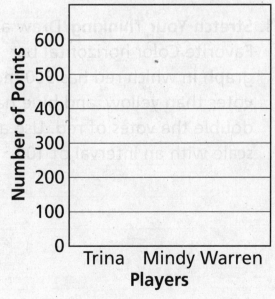

Remembering

Multiply or divide to find the unknown numbers.

1. $16 = \underline{\hspace{1cm}} \times 4$

2. $\underline{\hspace{1cm}} = 4 \times 8$

3. $42 \div 7 = \underline{\hspace{1cm}}$

4. $8 = 56 \div \underline{\hspace{1cm}}$

5. $2 \times \underline{\hspace{1cm}} = 10$

6. $9 \times 3 = \underline{\hspace{1cm}}$

Use the horizontal bar graph to answer each question.

7. How many markers are there?

   _____

8. How many more crayons are there than pencils?

   _____

9. How many fewer pencils are there than markers?

   _____

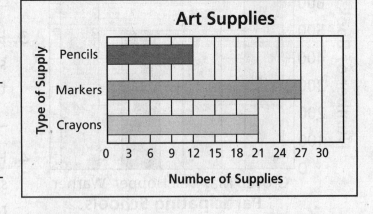

10. Write your own question that can be answered using the graph.

    _____

    _____

11. **Stretch Your Thinking** Draw a Favorite Color horizontal bar graph in which red has 300 more votes than yellow, and blue has double the votes of red. Use a scale with an interval of 100.

Read and Create Bar Graphs with Multidigit Numbers

Homework

The coach of the girls' soccer team measured the heights of the players to the nearest $\frac{1}{2}$ inch. She recorded the heights in the line plot below.

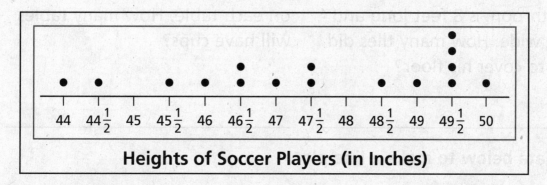

Heights of Soccer Players (in Inches)

Use the line plot to solve the problems.

1. How many players are $47\frac{1}{2}$ inches tall?

_____

2. What is the difference in height between the tallest player on the team and the shortest player?

_____

3. What is the most frequent height?

_____

4. How many players are on the soccer team?

_____

5. Are there more players $47\frac{1}{2}$ inches tall and greater or less than $47\frac{1}{2}$ inches tall?

_____

6. How many more players are $49\frac{1}{2}$ inches than $46\frac{1}{2}$ inches tall?

_____

Remembering

Write an equation and solve the problem.

1. Jon used 1-foot square tiles to cover his bathroom floor. The bathroom is 8 feet long and 10 feet wide. How many tiles did he use to cover his floor?

2. The principal buys 42 red cups and 21 blue cups. She puts 7 cups on each table. How many tables will have cups?

_____

Use the data below to make a line plot.

3.

Lengths of Pencils in Inches			
Lizzie	$7\frac{1}{2}$	Carl	6
Mario	5	Aja	6
Jenn	$6\frac{1}{2}$	Joe	$7\frac{1}{2}$
Travis	7	Jung	7
Karen	6	Terrell	7

Pencil Lengths

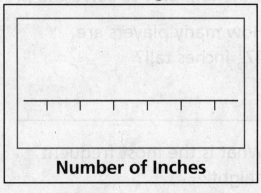

Number of Inches

4. Stretch Your Thinking You need to find the height of most third graders at your school. What type of data display would you use? Explain.

_____

_____

_____

Homework

Measure the length of a smile of 10 different people to the nearest $\frac{1}{2}$ inch.

1. Record the lengths in the box below.

_____
_____
_____
_____
_____
_____
_____
_____
_____

2. Organize the measurement data in a frequency table and a line plot.

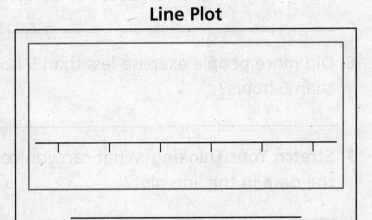

Frequency Table	
Length	**Tally**

Line Plot

3. Describe what your line plot shows.

_____

_____

Remembering

Write an equation and solve the problem.

1. There are 72 skateboards in the shop. If Todd sells 8 each day, how many days will it take him to sell all of the skateboards?

_____

Complete.

2. $36 = $ _____ $\times 4$ 3. _____ $\times 9 = 81$ 4. _____ $= 54 \div 6$

Use the line plot to solve the problems.

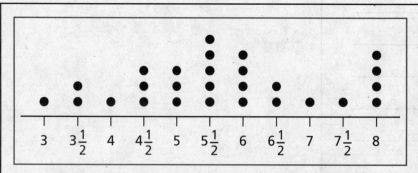

Time in Hours of Exercising for 1 Week

5. How many people exercised for 6 hours?

_____

6. Did more people exercise less than 5 hours or more than 6 hours?

_____

7. **Stretch Your Thinking** What can you conclude about the data in the line plot?

_____

_____

Focus on Mathematical Practices